Lost in Familiar Places

Lost in Familiar Places

Creating New Connections

between the Individual and Society

Edward R. Shapiro and A. Wesley Carr

Yale University Press ○ New Haven & London

AKI 2088- 1/4
STM- 515M

Published with assistance from the foundation established in memory
of Amasa Stone Mather of the Class of 1907, Yale College

Designed by Jill Breitbarth.
Set in Sabon and Gill Sans types by Marathon Typography Service,
Inc., Durham, North Carolina.
Printed in the United States of America by BookCrafters, Inc.,
Chelsea, Michigan.

Library of Congress Cataloging-in-Publication Data

Shapiro, Edward R., 1941–
Lost in familiar places : creating new connections between the
individual and society / Edward R. Shapiro and A. Wesley Carr.
p.   cm.
Includes bibliographical references and index.
ISBN 0-300-04947-1 (cloth)
      0-300-05787-3 (pbk.)
1. Social psychology.   2. Organizational behavior.   3. Family
treatment.   I. Carr, A. Wesley, 1941–   .   II. Title.
HM251.S459   1991
302—dc20   90-19662
                                                                CIP

The paper in this book meets the guidelines for permanence and
durability of the Committee on Production Guidelines for Book
Longevity of the Council on Library Resources.

10 9 8 7 6 5 4 3 2

For Roger L. Shapiro and Eric J. Miller

FOUR-YEAR-OLD SON: Mommy, I'd like to see the world start all over again.
MOTHER: Why?
SON: Because then I could see what it's like inside of you.
—Reported by a family

The potential space between baby and mother, between child and family, between individual and society or the world, depends on experience which leads to trust. It can be looked upon as sacred to the individual in that it is here that the individual experiences creative living.
—D. W. Winnicott, *Playing and Reality*

Contents

Preface

The task we set ourselves when we began this book was to consider how individuals might begin to cope with the experience of being lost amid the rapidly changing structures of contemporary social life. Initially, the task was interesting, if a bit academic. Through the process of writing, occasionally together but more often apart, we found the ideas themselves to be increasingly demanding and their implications upsetting. During the three years or so that we have worked on this book, each of us has assumed new roles in changing institutions. The experience of being lost became increasingly personal. The writing, therefore, has also become more intensely relevant to us. We hope this immediacy comes through to the reader.

The attempt to survey the emotions experienced in family and organizational life lays us open to a range of criticisms, and no doubt many will be justified. We have written from the perspectives of our own specific disciplines for those readers who—whatever their profession, discipline, or background—seek to comprehend the internal and external disarray that characterizes much of contemporary Western life. The study that initially brought us together, an exploration of human relations in groups and organizations, provides a significant and powerful model for thinking about and working in any field for it allows one to assess the actual and potential impact of the context on individuals. One piece of evidence for this statement lies in our own ability to collaborate without compromising either psychiatry or theology. A psychoanalyst/family researcher from the United States and a priest from the English church make an unusual pair. The psychoanalyst comes from a position in close relation to the data of the individual's internal life and, in his role as investigator of family life, to the data of shared family experience. The priest comes from a social system where there is a close connection between church and state and thus carries within his role a wider view of central human organizations in relationship to the larger society. The joining of the two perspectives forms the framework for the ideas presented. We hope this book will be a contribution to interdisciplinary learning.

Two of our mentors and friends have honored us by accepting the dedication of this book. Roger Shapiro, a psychoanalyst, was first exposed to group relations work when Margaret Rioch, a psychologist, invited Kenneth Rice from the Tavistock Institute of Human Relations to bring the Leicester model of group relations study to the United States in 1965. Roger carried the insights gained through his work with the Leicester model into his own seminal work on the study of families and adolescents at the National Institute of Mental Health (Scharff 1989). One of us (ERS) trained and worked with Roger in that setting and elsewhere. The other (AWC) participated in group relations conferences in Chelmsford, England, that Roger directed. We have both been influenced by his thinking, his gentleness, his sensitivity, and his ability to expand and continue an interpretive inquiry.

Eric Miller is Consultant and Director of the Group Relations Training Programme at the Tavistock Institute for Human Relations. Through the "Leicester Conferences" (Miller 1989), with which he has been involved since 1959, he has influenced a generation of those who have come to learn about unconscious processes in groups and organizations. One of us (AWC) has worked with Eric in various contexts, and both of us have been stimulated by his incisiveness. Many of the central concepts employed in this book—primary task, role, consultancy, systems, organization—are elaborated in his writing, first with A. Kenneth Rice (Miller and Rice 1967) and later in a series of papers and books. We will be delighted if we have achieved some of his clarity of thought and expression. This dedication is a small acknowledgment of Roger's and Eric's generosity with both their time and their minds.

Since we write from a tradition of collaborative work, we feel, like Freud, that "It remains an open question . . . how much the individual thinker or writer owes to the stimulation of the group in which he lives, and whether he does more than perfect a mental work in which the others have had a simultaneous share" (Freud 1921, p. 83). We hope that our effort does our friends the honor of building constructively on the study of human behavior to which they both have contributed so much.

Acknowledgments

Like any book, ours has emerged from engagement with the thoughts, ideas, and, indeed, lives of many. Some are mentioned by name in the course of the argument, others remain anonymous. One person deserves special mention: we both owe much to Margaret Rioch, whose hospitality and critical insights we have often enjoyed.

Shervert Frazier provided a unique and unencumbered setting for the exploration of divergent ideas at McLean Hospital in Boston; his sponsorship of this work over the past fifteen years has been both generous and stimulating. The late Richard Herrick provided a similar context at The Chelmsford Cathedral Centre for Research and Training in England. The staff, families, and trainees of the Adolescent and Family Treatment and Study Center at McLean and the staff and members of group relations conferences sponsored by the A. K. Rice Institute and the Tavistock Institute of Human Relations have stimulated our thinking, and their contributions are represented in these pages.

Donna Elmendorf took in our ideas and helped us to face and articulate their implications. In addition, the following individuals have struggled with us as we contemplated these notions, and we discover bits of their thinking as we reflect on what we have taken in from them: Adrienne Bentman, David Berkowitz, Peggy Chapman, Judith Freedman, Arthur Klein, Jonathan Kolb, James Krantz, Lynne Lieberman, Peter Marshall, Wendy Rosen, Leon Shapiro, Kathleen Pogue White, Karen Williams, and John Zinner.

Our families tolerated (on the whole with patience and good humor) three shared summer vacations as well as many visits on both sides of the Atlantic. Anne Dhu Shapiro and Jacob often managed time with Natalie Carr and Helga so that we could work. We are grateful for the generosity with which they endured the process of writing and for all the help they gave, not least when they chanted a very funny and original fugue about our work to sustain our morale.

Introduction

We live in a time of rapid and escalating social and environmental change. Our ability to position ourselves comfortably within our social contexts has been disturbed. In the past, reliable, inherited traditions and institutions—in the structure of families, the makeup of work settings and organizations, the familiar fabric of our social and political lives—helped us organize our experiences and make them recognizable. Now, social complexity and turbulence contribute to the bewilderment each of us feels as a once reliable and meaningful environment is completely transformed.

In the summer of 1983, for example, the trustees of the Massachusetts General Hospital, a Harvard Medical School affiliated institution, voted to explore the possibility of selling the hospital's nonprofit psychiatric institution (McLean Hospital) to a profit-making chain. The proposed sale would have relieved many of Massachusetts General's serious financial problems, permitting the funding of needed professorships and the renovation of outdated buildings at McLean. The trustees, serious men deeply commited to quality, anticipated no opposition from the medical staff at McLean, who, they felt, were not particularly interested in such practical matters. Their view was justified by the level of involvement in the hospital the medical staff had previously displayed. Most of the doctors had private practices along with their university duties. The board of trustees did not include members of the hospital staff, who constituted their own professional body within the hospital.

On returning from their summer vacations, the medical staff found their organization dramatically changed. Faced with the trustees' plan for reorganization and sale of the hospital, they felt confused, lost, and disorganized. The institution's familiar structure had been suddenly altered, and they could not simply resume their previous roles. The ensuing controversy was marked by the polarized views trustees and faculty had of each other. The doctors were considered ivory tower academics who did not understand the real world; the trustees were characterized as money-grubbing businessmen who understood neither the fragility of an academic operation nor the needs of patients.

Within three months, the seemingly apathetic medical faculty had mobilized itself, mounted an organized opposition, and convinced Harvard Medical School's faculty committee and the dean not to support the trustees' proposal. This unexpected response resulted from a shared but not previously articulated perception that members of the faculty, to their surprise, discovered through their discussions. According to this shared perception, the primary task of a medical institution should be to provide care to patients, not to make money. In addition, they believed that a commitment to profit would conflict with the necessary academic freedom to search for new ideas. In responding to a written questionnaire circulated among the faculty by a group from the McLean staff, many said that the two or three hours a week they spent at the hospital were the most important of their professional careers. Though many had previously felt isolated in the institutional context, they now discovered that it was in this setting that their highest values were expressed. The discussion triggered by the trustees' decision had exposed the shared beliefs and values that lay at the heart of the institution.

There was an obvious conflict of values between the different parties to the discussion. But as the argument developed, it became clear that the institution itself, the idea behind the hospital, represented important beliefs and values for each of the groups. For people in widely different roles, the hospital stood for aspects of themselves and their relationships with others in a way they had not previously grasped or articulated. The proposed changes to the hospital were not felt to be simply economic or political. They went far deeper and created a profoundly emotional response in the members of the institution.

This story is not so unusual. Many people today, whatever their roles within or responsibilities for their organizations, experience previously familiar social institutions as unstable. Affected by rapidly changing conditions, complex institutions seem to have moved beyond our capacity to comprehend them. Whether in factories or professional associations, and whatever the level of their formal involvement in the decision-making process, people often feel that major decisions that profoundly affect their lives are being made without their input.

This bewilderment is clearly apparent in a fundamental social institution like the family. Divorce, reconstitution of diverse family-like groups, and new reproductive methods have altered the form, content, and meaning of family life. Far from providing a natural or instinctive refuge for those pressured by other organizations or by life itself, the family has become yet another source of pressure. Both families and organizations —familiar places in which we live—have recently become strange. People are stressed by the sense of being lost, unable to find their way. Connections that once seemed reliable are missing.

Previous generations have also experienced changes in their world. In some countries, in the United States, for example, rapid social change has even been the model upon which a national culture was founded. But today, throughout Western societies, two phenomena exist that both contribute to social change and alter the ways we think about our experiences. These phenomena are the creation of various psychotherapies and the development of sophisticated biomedical means for controlling emotions, and they have sparked a widespread new search for ways of interpreting and managing emotional life. Some people have carried out this search professionally as teachers, researchers, or clinicians; others have undergone therapy or taken medication in the hope of learning about themselves and discovering ways to manage their chaotic experience. All of us, however, have been affected by the assumptions about the significance of our emotional lives that this revolution has unleashed.

A diversification of investigations in sociology and allied disciplines has paralleled these therapeutic developments. And group phenomena have also been well studied. Far from clarifying the confusion, however, the human sciences have seemed to polarize the individual and the group. Therapy and medication are offered to individuals. Group therapy is similarly envisioned as a means of helping the individual. Yet efforts to describe how groups and organizations function as entities (so-called human systems analysis) regularly discount the significance of the individual. And although attempts have been made (beginning with Freud himself) to interpret social activity on the basis of insights derived from individual analysis, these have not been widely accepted (Freud 1930). Nonetheless, the availability of in-depth analysis of the individual coupled with the increasing recognition through sociological study of the degree to which we live through collaborative endeavor now require that we attempt to create a coherent way of interpreting contemporary life from both these perspectives—the individual and the social.

INDIVIDUALS AND THEIR CONTEXTS

"The individual is the creature of the group, the group of the individual" (Miller and Rice 1967, p. 17). Our individual lives are lived in a series of groups. Some of these groups are obvious and immediate—a family, a club, a class at school, a neighborhood, a work organization. Others are more amorphous—the nation, a religious tradition, a professional association. Life in the first set is marked by face-to-face contact. The problems that arise are frequently described as matters of communication: How shall I talk to my neighbor or colleague? The second set of groups usually have a less obvious impact on our day-to-day existence, but when they do—at a time of national emergency or during profound personal anxiety, such as a birth or death—they exercise a powerful influence.

Within these groups individuals are faced with the task of defining themselves, adjusting their distinctive personalities, and establishing identities-in-context, identities that can stand for deeply (and often unconsciously) held values and beliefs. This task is made more complex by the variety of changing roles we are required to adopt in our social institutions. The more modern psychotherapy makes us aware of our personal complexity within the new world, the more we see that our self-definition is formed within social institutions and among the chronic uncertainties and ambiguities of social interaction. We find ourselves having to affirm our personhood in a range of increasingly tumultuous settings.

Awash, therefore, in a sea of complex and overlapping contexts, we tend to lose hope of being able to grasp anything at all. We are less confident in who we are as persons and what our various roles are. A sense of personal significance and meaning eludes us in the swirl of social change. And if the family, a primary institution, is not a place where we can be confident in our basic roles as male or female, parent or child, husband or wife, then what roles *can* we discover for ourselves with any confidence?

SOME KEY CONCEPTS

In this new and unfamiliar context, the questions we must ask have changed. No longer is the individual query sufficient: "How can I make sense of my own life and the various roles I take up?" As our example about the hospital illustrates, a larger and more socially significant issue needs to be addressed and will be explored in this book:

"Can we develop a shared interpretation of experience? And if so, how?" An approach to collaborative interpretation might allow each of us to discover our connections to those contexts for human experience that are larger than ourselves. Such connections would allow for a shared perspective that transcends the individual, joining him[1] to others and relieving the perplexing sense of being lost amidst the rapidly changing (and largely uninterpreted) structures of contemporary society. Creating such connections between ourselves and these structures would inevitably lead to a more coherent and meaningful sense of society as a whole.

Interpretation, a key notion in our argument, will be used and explored throughout the book. We use this concept to refer to ideas that provide connections, meanings, or a way of comprehending previously unrelated experiential data. More specifically, in this book we will be talking about shared or *negotiated* interpretation. Each of us has an interpretive stance—a way of making sense of our reality. We do not often listen to others' interpretations and ponder how their interpretations are right for them and how their interpretations connect to ours. Even less frequently do we discover how these linked interpretations relate to a larger context that joins us all. Acceptance of the potential validity of individual interpretations and discovery of the connections to a larger context is our interpretive stance.

When people work or live in any communal enterprise (a family, an organization), they develop individual interpretations of their experiences. Noticing that they belong to a collective entity that includes others may allow them to recognize that others may have different interpretations, including different feelings and thoughts. Thus, joint interpretation of shared experience involves negotiation. It is not a process whereby one person or group imposes an interpretation on others (as the trustees appeared to do to the staff with their plan to sell the hospital).

There are two major (and in many ways problematic) consequences of the use of interpretation. First, any approach to interpreting human experience must take uncertainty into account. Second, the irrational dimension of human behavior cannot be discounted. It follows that we cannot claim to "understand" social and organizational behavior—the term is too final and too certain. These phenomena can, however, be grasped or "interpreted" collectively if we can agree upon the relevant context for that interpretation. A shared context, as we shall see, will itself require negotiation. For example, in the hospital described in our opening story, the trustees saw the pressures as arising from the institution's financial needs, whereas for the medical staff the problems involved the hospital's tasks of treatment and academic research. The two groups had not agreed upon a common frame of reference for interpreting their difficulties.

For individual interpretation, our basic frame of reference is our own experience. If I experience something, I believe that I know it for myself, given the referent of my accumulated experiences of life and knowledge of my own body and mind. There are difficulties about this assumption, but these are insignificant by comparison with the question of how we get to any shared referent that joins people in linked, deepening interpretations of their interactive human behavior.

We spend much of our lives in collaborative efforts with others—that is, in organizations of some kind. And it is in these collective entities that confusion about the interpretation of our experiences emerges, requiring us to negotiate collaborative meaning. In organizational life, one opening position for negotiated interpretation might be something like this: "Given that we agree that we are engaged in a particular task, how can we attempt to make sense of the behavior we are observing and experiencing *in relation to it?*" For example, the trustees and medical staff in our story initially disagreed on the institution's task. If, however, both groups agreed that the hospital's *primary* task was to provide care to patients, they might unite to examine their different pressures and to work at this task from their different perspectives. A shared frame of reference provides a partial shelter from unrelenting ambiguity and uncertainty and the danger of idiosyncratic points of view. In an ambiguous and uncertain world, such shelters are not easy to come by and are to be treasured.

The place where we begin to ask questions about joint interpretation is the family. The paradigm for our argument is interaction within the family, looked at not just as the behavior of a collection of individuals but also as a structured whole. Our basic premise is that individuals carry with them a model for organizational life that is derived from their early family experiences and their roles within the family. They learn customary ways of relating to authority, listening to the experiences of others, and collaborating around shared tasks. As we shall see, they also learn ways of handling internal conflict by disconnecting psychologically from other family members. By examining case studies of disturbed families, we will illuminate certain key concepts that describe our interactions with others in organizations. One such concept is *projective identification*, a psychological mechanism through which individuals dissociate from unbearable aspects of their own experiences, irrationally and unwittingly inducing them in others. Projective identification will be described in detail in chapter 2.

Another essential concept is the *holding environment*, a notion that describes the management of emotional aspects of family life. In the healthy family's holding environment, empathic interpretation, valuing the experiences of others, and containment of aggression and sexuality combine to sustain the integrity of the family unit and make the development of the individual possible.

Two additional notions — *task* and *role* — are fundamental to our argument and are examined at several points in the book. Briefly, "task" is what an organization, whether a family or some larger unit, must perform in order to continue to exist. Often, of course, there is more than one task, and they compete for primacy. In the family, for example, the tasks include economic survival, the formation of collaborative values, and facilitating the development of its individual members. "Role" describes the particular function of the overall task assigned to or taken up by any individual. In the family, for example, we may speak of the role of father, mother, or child. Without the prior notion of "family," such role descriptions are meaningless. And without some sense of the task of a family, they lack content. We shall focus here on the developmental task. Our observations indicate that if the family ceases to work at this task, it begins to disintegrate and family members begin to show pathological symptoms. These, however, cannot be treated only as individual disturbance. They are, at least in part, the product of the loss of a shared sense of task, with the result that the people involved also lose a sense of their role.

To understand our experiences in a role, we need to be able to scrutinize them objectively. To have an experience and at the same time study it has been referred to as *participant-observation*. In anthropological field work and in American psychiatry, this method has led to many insights about the culture one is living in, whether it be a tribal culture in a foreign land or a psychological culture that our patients create with us (Devereux 1967). Using this role of participant-observer, we shall examine the holding environment of the family as an organization.

Through a brief examination of the connections between the family as primary organization and the various types of organizations in which we live, we come to the core of our argument: a negotiated *interpretive stance* provides us with a way of engaging with and making sense of organizational complexity and our own place and worth as individuals within it. This stance contains three basic components, of equal importance: the use of individual experience, the irreducible basis on which we all operate; the collaborative testing of reality; and the discovery of a larger context to which our linked experiences relate.

Part I

Learning from

the Family

In the following four chapters, we examine the family as a paradigmatic institution for organizations generally. Through this study we develop the basic concepts that we shall apply in our later investigation— individual experience, projective identification, the holding environment, and the way in which the perspective of the participant-observer (whether therapist or consultant) may enable him to tolerate and use his complex feelings as data for developing larger interpretations. Our focus is on the disturbed family. Just as the study of individual medical pathology led to the recognition of the basic structures of healthy human functioning and development, so it is with the pathology of families. When the family is in trouble the underlying mechanisms for sustaining its psychological health are most in evidence. These mechanisms, we shall argue, can also be discerned in other interactive groups and organizations.

1 ○ Listening to Human Experience: The Importance of Interpersonal Curiosity

The family is the first and most basic organization we all encounter. Within the framework of the family, we can develop the skills we need for competent organizational behavior. The most important skill is the capacity to learn from individual experiences, our own and others'. The study of disrupted families provides clues to the development of this essential ability.

The clinical study and treatment of families has revealed one trait to be the hallmark of psychological health and stability: curiosity. The effects of its absence in disturbed families are profound; the reasons for its development, or failure of development, are perplexing; and its cultivation as an element of treatment is critical.

In many families where individuals manifest severe personal problems, the members have a striking lack of curiosity about one another. Instead, they are often remarkably certain that they know, understand, and can speak for other family members without further discussion. If individual members attempt to challenge assertions about who they are, they encounter bland denial, unshakable conviction, or platitudinous reassurance. Even though such assertions are usually incorrect and frequently lead to escalating disagreements within the family, this cycle is often difficult to interrupt.

In infants, curiosity is a manifestation of an inborn instinct to learn (Freud 1905; Nunberg 1961). Later, it becomes integrated into the child's personality and contributes to an interest in the experiences of others. Without curiosity and an empathic interest in other people, an individ-

ual can have difficulty developing a mature capacity for love and intimacy. And if these capacities are not fully developed, individuals have
difficulty functioning well as parents. Parents who are curious about
their child's experience of the world encourage the child to describe his
experience and to distinguish it from the views held by others. Through
this process, the child develops personal *boundaries*, a concept we will
refer to frequently throughout the book.

In essence, when parents ask their child, "What is your experience?"
they authorize the child to *have* a separate experience and allow an
implicit boundary to form between child and parent. On one side of this
boundary is the child's experience of himself; on the other side are the
parents' views of him. This stable personal boundary constitutes a key
element in healthy growth and development, since secure self-awareness
allows a child to have flexible interactions with other people.

The parents' capacity for empathic interpretation and their ability to
respond with confidence and knowledge based on their own experience
when the child is anxious and confused are important elements of good
parenting. Their confidence communicates to the child a picture of a
secure external world. But in many disturbed families, parents appear to
be prematurely certain about their child and his *internal* world. They act
as if they have (and sometimes explicitly claim) a total understanding of
the child's experience. This excessive parental certainty can interfere with
the child's development and often provides a false support based more
on the parents' needs to manage their own anxiety than on an accurate
interpretation of the child's concerns. The parents' lack of openness and
curiosity contributes to feelings of isolation, emptiness, and futility within
the family group.

Such isolation, a classical instance of being lost in a familiar place, is
not limited to dysfunctional families. Excessive "certainty" is a recognizable element within all human organizations; it contributes to the
disconnection of the individuals lost within them.

INTERPERSONAL CURIOSITY AND THE
EARLIEST YEARS

The baby's active curiosity manifests itself in his efforts to feel,
smell, and mouth everything within reach. The child's interpersonal curiosity, however, is limited during early infancy by his concern with himself. Psychoanalytic inferences suggest that the infant does not yet perceive that the mother has an independent existence (A. Freud 1965).

Instead, the infant perceives her as an aspect of his own experience of himself, usually in terms of a role the baby assigns to her within the framework of his needs and wishes.

One outcome of this perception is that the infant seems to transform the mother's concerns with other members of the family, with work, or with outside interests, as well as her depressions, illnesses, and absences, into rejection and desertion. But these feelings do not inevitably carry negative consequences. For during this period, while the child experiences his mother with certainty as a part of himself, her legitimate concerns contribute to the child's first steps in separation and the beginnings of an individual sense of self. As the infant begins to recognize that the mother is another genuinely separate person, the original infantile certainty shifts toward a capacity for interpersonal curiosity. But before such separateness is achieved, the child is preoccupied with himself and is painfully certain that he knows why his mother is doing things to him: it must be, so he feels, because he is "good" or "bad."

In order to manage these feelings, the infant reshapes his frustrating experience by projecting his own anger and aggression onto others. He then feels that he is the victim of mother's hatred, resents it, and acts upon it. As the child matures in a sufficiently secure parental environment, he begins to experience his anger at the limitations of the maternal response and gradually dares to notice that he is angry at his beloved mother. When she emotionally survives his anger—when she remains interested, sufficiently accessible, and potentially loving—she demonstrates to the child her independent existence. The child, in turn, can begin to recognize both his loving and his angry feelings toward one and the same mother, who both gratifies and frustrates him. This critical step in development leads him to recognize and to some extent be in charge of ambivalent feelings.

The mother's ability to aid her child in this process is determined by the extent to which she can remain open to all responses from her child, whether she feels them to be good or bad. Having a child who projects into her in this fashion reawakens her own earliest impulses. If she can tolerate these impulses in herself, she can remain reliably responsive to similar impulses in her child without withdrawing or retaliating.

For instance, at the end of a long day, when the mother is exhausted, irritable, and upset, she offers her infant her breast; he screams and refuses to take it. The infant's rejection of her and her own identification with him evoke her childhood recollection of feeling unaccepted and unloved by her own parents. At this moment, the mother has an unconscious choice: she may confuse the image of her child with that of her parent and react with the rage this overlapping experience and memory evoke in her; or she may suspend her reaction long enough to consider the possibility that the infant's rejection is precipitated by something other than her inadequacy, something within her child that remains unknown to her. In this moment of suspension, many facets of the mother's maturity are tested: her tolerance of frustration, her capacity to live with uncertainty, her acceptance of ambivalence and separation anxiety, her confidence in her own boundaries and consequent testing of reality ("This is an infant; it is not my parents"), her capacity to observe and to refuse to respond immediately and unthinkingly, and her curiosity about and interest in her child.[1]

This ideal mother, of course, does not exist. Fortunately, however, our growth to maturity as individuals does not depend upon having perfect mothers: they only have to be "good enough." The "good enough mother" (Winnicott 1960b) responds automatically in a complex manner. On the one hand, she allows herself to recall the sensation of being poorly loved (in this instance, not well fed) and grasp this aspect of her own child's response. This perception allows her to both evaluate her own actions ("Am I being unaccepting?") and comfort her distressed child. On the other hand, she is also able to suspend her conviction about the accuracy of her empathic interpretation (that is, suspend her certainty) in order to provide her child an opportunity to define himself in his own way, with his own capabilities. The mother functions here in a paradigmatic participant-observer role that we described in the introduction as the capacity to be in one's role and study it at the same time.

Clearly at crucial moments it is essential for the mother *not* to know too well what the child needs. During these periods, the parent who can tolerate uncertainty and remain open to new information provides the child with an implicit message that some territory belongs exclusively to the child and remains totally in his control. This parent communicates the limits of her omniscience and offers the child the freedom to create his own internal world, which he can ultimately, at his own volition, choose to share with the parent and others.

Parents who are unable to tolerate the ambiguity, uncertainty, and relative helplessness of this stance often struggle anxiously to control their interactions with the child. Parental outbursts of child abuse are not infrequently precipitated by the child's efforts to hold onto a separate experience. For example, a child may be upset because of difficulties with friends or at school and may withhold information about these difficulties from parents because he feels ashamed and vulnerable. Or, a child may be upset for reasons he cannot articulate. Such withholding or unresponsiveness may challenge a parent's need for omnipotent control. Vulnerable parents, overwhelmed by tense interactions with their child that they can neither control nor understand, may react with anxious aggression, telling the child in effect, "If I can't understand what is upsetting you, then I will do something to you so that you (and I) will *know* what you're crying about."

Ideally, parents will be able to communicate to the child their continuing interest in him and their ability to tolerate the relative impotence, ambiguity, and uncertainty that result from their acknowledging the child's separateness. An intimate relationship with such a parent provides the child with a model of creative relationships. Taking these parental attitudes into himself and making them his own enable him to tolerate impulses and sustain new ideas and information about other people and their experiences. Those whose healthy upbringing has allowed them to develop stable self boundaries are able to construct accurate images of others that are continually reshaped as new information is perceived and integrated (Shapiro 1978a).

If, however, the child's normal infantile experience is constricted by unresolved parental conflicts, aspects of which are projected onto the child, the parents will become convinced that their perceptions of their child are correct. These rigid parental perceptions may cause the child to constrict his sense of himself in self-defense. Motivated in part by his need to protect his parents from anxiety, the child may develop a "false self" and behave as if he were the child his parents need rather than the child he is (Winnicott 1960a).

The formation of this shell, or false self, in response to the unempathic intrusions of others is one way (a pathological, noninterpretive way) to manage the experience of being lost in a familiar place. The creation of a false self, which hinges on *both* the parents' pathological certainty and the child's willingness (unconscious) to sacrifice his true self to his parents' needs, illuminates the existence of a third aspect of the parent-child relationship: the "parent-child unit." The parent-child unit transcends both parent and child and describes the context within which their relationship develops. It is the first place where meaning is negotiated with others even before we can articulate it.

A CASE STUDY IN BOUNDARY FORMATION

So far, the discussion has revolved around the importance and nature of interpersonal curiosity in the earliest years. We now wish to demonstrate how it can remain a central issue through later developmental stages. A case study from an individual psychoanalysis will demonstrate the dangers inherent in the seductive notion of "understanding."

As an adolescent, a schizoid patient wrote in her diary that one basic rule for living was never to tell people more than they could understand. The youngest child of a depressed mother, she felt her mother demonstrated a "pseudo-curiosity" about her. When she was upset, her mother would insist that they discuss the girl's problems, for, as her mother put it, "talking helps." Yet, if she then attempted to describe her feelings, her mother would attempt to "cheer her up" and offer platitudes rather than actively listening. The girl described this experience as "like speaking in an empty room," recognizing that her mother's preoccupation with her own depression made her unavailable to her daughter.

This patient's "basic rule" revealed her desperate attempt to protect herself from a repetition of this experience of emotional abandonment. She decided to tell her mother only what her mother could grasp emotionally. As a consequence the patient studied her mother and developed an overexpanded capacity to be sensitive to others' needs to the exclusion of attending to her own. She was hypersensitive to so-called supportive comments from those around her. If someone said, "I understand," her response was not to feel accepted but rather to feel isolated and emotionally abandoned. She knew that such "understanding" could not possibly be accurate since she never revealed enough of herself for anyone to understand. Similarly, a so-called supportive comment like "That must have been hard for you" evoked in her feelings not of comfort and relief but of panic and obliteration, since she perceived it as an *instruction* to feel that it was "hard" for her. If she felt differently, she believed that her feelings would not be accepted.

Through analysis, the patient's own contributions to those experiences could be examined. As her relationship to the analyst intensified, she developed a fixed perception that he was not interested in her and did not believe or accept her. Her oversensitivity to minor cues — his silence, shifting in his chair, occasional premature interventions — convinced her that her perception was accurate. With continual clarification of her own fear of presenting herself and her feelings, however, she began to recognize that her interpretations of the analyst's intent were based on paltry evidence. She began to realize that she was not interested in herself and that she was responding to the analyst with the same kind of pathological certainty she had experienced from her mother.

Because of the patient's sensitivity, the analyst needed to monitor closely his responses to her projections. This enabled him to distinguish the patient's projections from accurate perceptions and made it possible for him to reveal to the patient her certainty that she could "read" his hateful intent despite the lack of data. These clarifications helped her to recognize that her fantasies originated within herself and to perceive the boundary between her own experience of reality and the analyst's separate and unknowable experience.

During the first two years of the analysis, the patient developed an increasingly complex view of her childhood experience. This development was most graphically evident in the sequential analysis of a dream she presented in the first year. In this dream, the patient's father cut up a watermelon and gave her the smallest piece. Her initial associations revealed her fury at both the analyst and her father for not asking her how much she wanted and for not reading her mind and knowing that she wanted more. She associated this dream with childhood memories of both parents telling her what she wanted without checking with her.

As the patient became better able to acknowledge her own wishes and emotions, she realized that in the dream she had not *told* her father how much she wanted and that he could not, therefore, have known. She recognized that her fear of *noticing* how much she wanted (and of noticing her anger at possible frustration) contributed to her feeling that others should know her wishes without her having to take responsibility for informing them. She recalled that the largest piece of melon in the dream had been given to her mother and then began to recognize her anger and competitiveness with her mother and her fury at her father for his limited involvement with her.

This patient was confused between what she felt she *must* have (complete understanding without communication) and what she *wished* to have (a more intimate relationship with her father). This confusion is characteristic of patients who have difficulty recognizing their separateness from others. The boundaries around their experience of themselves remain tenuous and easily become lost when the needs of others intrude. These patients have serial relationships in which they continually attempt to ascertain the needs of those around them and to accommodate themselves to fit those needs. Their own separate experiences of genuineness, depth, and complexity remain unavailable.

INTERPERSONAL CURIOSITY IN CHILDHOOD
AND ADOLESCENCE

Successful resolution of the earlier and necessary infantile fusion with the mother, with the resultant formation of intact boundaries surrounding a complex internal world, prepares the child for the oedipal period. This stage is marked by a need to model his further development on his identifications with his parents. The healthy oedipal child has a well-developed ability to define his own territory. If the parents do not set clear boundaries, the child's passion and assertiveness can lead him to invade the intimate parental relationship and inappropriately claim aspects of it as his own. It is the parents' task during this period to model for their child their own ability to create firm boundaries around themselves, both as a couple and as individuals, each with his or her own gender identity.

In healthy parents, these firm adult boundaries convey to the child that there are elements of the parental experience which he cannot know and from which he is excluded. The child's longing, envy, jealousy, and curiosity about the mysterious relations between the parents lie behind his subsequent active search for an idealized relationship with another person who represents the repository of this unknown, and heretofore unknowable, experience (Kernberg 1977).

Parents are often affected by the child's powerful sexual curiosity and interest. They may surrender the privacy of the marital relationship, either by getting involved in individual interactions with the child that actively exclude the other parent or by behaving defensively and superficially as a single undifferentiated parental unit. If, during this period, each parent maintains a separate identity as an adult sexual being who sustains individual interest in and engagement with the other, the parents provide the child with an essential model for the further development of his self-awareness. The parents' ability to develop shared views of the child and integrated responses to his needs allows the child to learn about the creation of meaning as a product of negotiated interpretation between people in a role (the parental role) in relation to a task (development). This knowledge enables him to join the interpretive complexity of the family group and thence the complexity of organizational life.

In adolescence, the demand for parental interest and flexibility is especially high. Since both the adolescent's mind and body are rapidly changing and developing, parental interest helps to provide the adolescent with the freedom to redefine himself continually as his adult identity evolves.

For some adolescents, their impoverished childhood experiences or the lack of parental support for their adolescent experience may interfere with normal individuation. Studies of the families of such adolescents suggest that the parental coalition is often unstable because one or both parents are burdened with unresolved childhood conflicts of their own.[2] These conflicts may blur the boundaries between the two parents and between parents and child. As a consequence, the entire family loses its capacity to negotiate shared meaning and interpretation in a mutually respectful way. The disturbed adolescent in such families appears to be chosen unconsciously, by both his parents and his siblings, to represent aspects of their unresolved conflicts.

For example, if the parents have unconscious anxiety about their own sexual impulses, they may see their child as ridden with such impulses. Or if they are in conflict about their own dishonesty, they may find themselves distrusting their child without any evidence for doing so. These mistaken perceptions can result in a shared family certainty about the adolescent. Such interactions have a profound impact on the adolescent's experience of himself and contribute to the further weakening of his unstable boundaries as well as supporting stereotyped patterns of behavior between the adolescent and other family members.

Pathological certainty in family life is stifling. Family members chronically exposed to such obliterating interactions develop stale, shallow, mechanical investments in themselves and each other. The thin social veneer in these families is often shattered by eruptions of violence, barely concealed contempt, or flight from the family itself.

Although inferences from therapeutic experience with troubled adult and adolescent patients may suggest the origins of some of our difficulties in adopting and sustaining an interpretive stance in our family lives, there remains a central difficulty in our argument. With regard to the link between parental interpersonal curiosity and the development of the child's self-experience, we must note that many deeply curious and well-adjusted individuals emerge within families where the parents are stolid, seemingly uncurious, and platitudinous. Therefore, we cannot extrapolate directly from these therapeutic observations to notions of adequate parenting.

Certain children appear to have the capacity to find other people in their lives (either in childhood or in later life) who offer them the needed interpersonal interactions through which to develop themselves and their ideas. Providing a forum for these interpersonal interactions may be one of the functions of a healthy organization. Unfortunately, such opportunities are not always available.

CURIOSITY, CERTAINTY, AND AN INTERPRETIVE STANCE

This exploration reveals an unmistakable connection between curiosity and the capacity for negotiated interpretation. At each stage of development curiosity enables the child to form, acknowledge, and use boundaries. Recognizing one's own boundaries enables one to make sense of personal experience and to negotiate the complexities of social interaction. Boundaries form the basis of our interpretive stance.

When we examine the individual in relation to the family, the importance of boundaries becomes fully apparent. Our case study and discussion indicate how, when, and why boundaries can become confused and how clarification can be facilitated by an outside point of reference (the analyst or therapist). Our everyday life, however, is more complex, and the outside point of reference is not so easily identifiable. An analyst or therapist is not always available to help clarify our confusion about our boundaries.

However, even in families where pathological certainty seems to be addressed only with outside intervention, the outsider is not in fact the point of reference. Although an outsider can provide a different perspective from those within the family group, he cannot simply work from within himself without also running the risk of developing his own pathological certainty. In collaborative work, all participants need a reference that goes beyond the self. This, we suggest, is provided by the context for the collaboration. Therapist, parents, and children all work together on a series of boundaries because they (whether they consciously realize it or not) are collaboratively engaged in a specific task.

Roger Shapiro and his colleagues at the National Institute of Mental Health (Shapiro and Zinner 1976; Scharff 1989) have suggested that the family's primary task is to promote the development of each of its members. To the extent that this provides an unconscious agenda for family members' collaborative or dysfunctional behavior, the interpretive stance does not simply become focused on producing a "cured" adolescent or a competent father or loving mother. Instead, the analysis focuses on clarifying roles and their relation to the family's task and on helping family members collaborate more effectively. And this focus on the collaborative task provides the link between our earliest development, our maturing, and our connectedness with our institutions.

2 ○ Living in the

First Organization

Our first experience of an organization occurs in the family. Whether this family is secure and well managed or fragile and disorganized, each of us begins life in some sort of family. In this chapter and in the next two chapters, we will study one family in some detail in order to illustrate the complementary dynamics of the individual and the family group. This examination will illuminate the need to include both if we hope to clarify the meaning of individual experience in context.

The case study involves a so-called borderline adolescent and her family. A generation ago, when the intact nuclear family was still widely assumed to be a stable institution in Western society, an institution holding many of society's core values, the diagnosis of "neurosis" was the familiar manifestation of psychopathology. Neurotic individuals experienced their conflicts as internal and presented themselves to psychiatrists with such *symptoms* as anxiety, guilt, and depression. Neurotics were able to manage in the world fairly competently and considered themselves the source of their difficulties. They had internalized a structure of personality that allowed them to take responsibility for their lives and to develop a complex fantasy life.

In contemporary society, where "family" has become a broader notion, less stable, less nuclear, and less predictable, the diagnosis of "borderline" is increasingly made (Kernberg 1975). These patients are characterized by *behavioral* problems. They are lost in a world of people they believe they know, have difficulty controlling their impulses and taking responsibility for themselves, and have a limited capacity to develop complex fantasy lives. They manage reasonably well in situations where external structure is provided, where limits and tasks are clear, authority is well delineated, and psychological interest and support are forthcoming. But in unstructured situations they become disorganized, act chaotically, and behave impulsively with poor judgment. They cannot tolerate anxiety and possess no clear goal orientation. Often they show no symptoms—that is, they do not complain of internally experienced bad feelings. They consider others the source of their problems, and people around them often have difficulty tolerating their behavior and their demands. In many ways, these patients have difficulty experiencing themselves as separate from others, and they have powerful needs for others to supply psychologically missing aspects of themselves. In other words, borderline patients are exquisitely sensitive to their interpersonal environment, which they find disruptive (Shapiro 1978a). Because they have been unable to develop an inner psychological structure that allows them to function well autonomously, they are extraordinarily vulnerable to any lack of structure in their external organizations.

The difficulties discovered in the families of borderline patients contribute to these patients' problems in developing autonomous functioning within the family group and in the world. We believe that these phenomena reveal a crucial aspect of organizational functioning under stress. Grasping these connections will clarify aspects of organizational life that have been obscure and not amenable to exploration.

PROJECTIVE IDENTIFICATION

The psychological mechanism called projective identification is a central bridging concept, linking our understanding of the psychological functioning of the individual with the transpersonal functioning of human systems. Initially described by Melanie Klein (1946) as an infant's fantasy in relation to the mother, the notion of projective identification has been elaborated in contemporary psychiatry—for example, by Kernberg (1975, 1976)—in connection with borderline psychopathology. Zinner and Shapiro (1975) enlarged its scope to refer to transactional phenomena in the families of adolescents. It has also been discerned in group interactions (Bion 1961).

Projective identification is a psychological mechanism by which the individual tries to manage an uncomfortable experience by dissociating from it and inducing similar feelings in another person with whom a continuing connection is established. For example, a person made anxious by his own temptation to steal might develop a relationship with another person whom he covertly tempts (by leaving money unattended) and then criticizes for being tempted. It is a ubiquitous phenomenon of interpersonal life, linking people in ways that are often beyond their awareness. Projective identification begins with an empathic sensitivity to the experience of others and carries this awareness a step further into a particular kind of relationship. All of the eight components of projection identification are further illustrated and elaborated in the subsequent discussion.

1. The projection or disavowal of an uncomfortable aspect of ourselves.

2. The discovery (through empathic resonance) of another person who has an attribute that corresponds to that aspect of ourselves that we are attempting to disavow.

3. The willingness, conscious or not, of the other person to accept the projected attribute as part of himself.

4. The development of an enduring relationship between ourselves and the other in which the projections are sustained by unconscious collusion.

5. The other (now seen as possessing the disavowed characteristics) is consciously identified as unlike the self, while an unconscious relationship is sustained in which the projected attribute can be experienced vicariously.

6. The use of manipulative behavior that is unconsciously designed to elicit feelings or behavior from the other to support the idea that the projected attribute belongs to him.

7. Selective inattention to any of the real aspects of the other person that may contradict or invalidate the projection.

8. A complementarity of projections — both participants project.

Projective identification is most easily discerned in couples. Though present in some form in all marriages, projective identification often becomes manifest when there is trouble. Couples who come for treatment often present themselves as unidimensional complementary stereotypes: one is frigid, the other lusty; one is generous, the other stingy; one is sociable, the other reclusive; and so forth. Because of the stress that lies behind these presentations, the complexity inherent in each individual is obscured by the defensive use of projective identification.

Take, for example, a couple described by Zinner (1976). Mr. A has aggressive strivings, longs to be taken care of, and experiences great conflict about his passivity. When placed in a passive position, he becomes anxious. Mrs. A has similar aggressive strivings and passive longings, but her major conflict concerns her guilt over the potential destructiveness of her aggression.

In their relationship, the couple has developed a complementary use of projective identification in which Mr. A is powerfully aggressive and Mrs. A extremely passive. Mr. A has no conflict about his aggression and is free to manifest it. His wife has a major conflict about her aggression so she disavows it and projects it onto her husband. She then behaves in such a way as to provoke his aggression, hates him for it, but maintains a covert identification with it.

Similarly, Mrs. A has no conflict about her passivity and is therefore free to experience it and manifest it. Her husband cannot stand his own passivity, so he projects it onto his wife, acts in such a way as to increase her passivity, is contemptuous of her for being passive, and unconsciously identifies with it.

Though this mechanism is useful in that it relieves each individual from conflict, projective identification results in rigidity and constriction in each member of the pair. Their complexity as individuals is restricted and they are heavily dependent on each other. For example, if Mrs. A were treated individually for her guilt so that she became freer to be aggressive, she might take the initiative in their sexual relationship. This would place Mr. A in a passive position, evoking conflict and anxiety in him, which might make him sexually impotent. In such a situation, there would be an improving wife but a symptomatic husband.

We have made this story simplistic and readily acknowledge that many other factors may be involved. But the observation of these dynamics allows us to see that important aspects of how people behave and interact are not specific to them as individuals alone. Projective identification and its use as an interpretive notion direct us to see both individuals and their interpersonal context simultaneously.

People are intrinsically complex. It is, therefore, likely that different interpersonal contexts will evoke strikingly different aspects of individuals. We cannot consider individuals apart from their contexts. The concept of projective identification is one means of facing this problem without surrendering the importance of individual autonomy or the reality that our lives are contextual. The family is a sufficiently small context in which the significance of each individual is in principle not in dispute. It is, therefore, a convenient (and familiar) place to begin to examine the nature of the interconnection between the individual and the group which, we shall suggest, is fundamental for grasping other facets of individual and social connectedness.

Given that the marital bond is probably grounded to some degree in projective identification, the birth of a child offers new possibilities for the partners to project their internal conflicts onto another individual or to experience in new ways previously disavowed aspects of themselves. This step beyond the pair brings us closer to the more complex interpersonal mechanisms that are characteristic of organizations. In the following presentation of the family of a borderline adolescent, our focus is on the dynamic tensions within and between individuals in particular roles within the family. These unconscious and unexposed dynamics subvert the family's task of development. We hope to illustrate how psychological pressures generated within individuals in the context of the family can coalesce to create family dysfunction. This may provide the basis for a model of organizational functioning that will allow us to grasp the increasingly problematic relationship between individuals and organizations.

CASE STUDY: PROJECTIVE IDENTIFICATION IN THE BIENEGRO FAMILY

Sarah Bienegro,[1] a nineteen-year-old female, was admitted to the hospital after a three-year history of running away, promiscuity, an illegitimate pregnancy and abortion, and drug abuse. Most serious, however, was her almost nightly abuse of alcohol to the point of unconsciousness. Her main complaint was that she found herself increasingly "spaced out," isolated, unable to talk or think clearly, and totally devoid of feeling. Her alcohol abuse was an attempt to treat herself for this isolation. She related, in a bland tone, how alcohol enabled her to change from being isolated and inhibited to being aggressive and outgoing. She was able to have sex only when drunk, often punching and biting her partner.

Sarah was unable to connect assertive and dependent aspects of her internal self in order to function well interpersonally. She could not have sex or consciously depend on another person without entering a dissociated state brought about by the use of alcohol. This pathological disconnection between aspects of herself can be understood in part as a product of transactions between Sarah and her parents, and in turn between them and their own parents. In attempting to reconstruct these relationships over three generations, we discovered a persistent difficulty in responding to dependent needs that are perceived as hostile, draining demands.

In reconstructing the history of Sarah's parents, we have to work without confirmatory witnesses from the past and without being able to observe them, individually or together. This, however, is not of immediate concern. We are interested in each parent's current perceptions of his or her original family. These perceptions reflect the data we have to deal with when trying to interpret the dynamics of the present family, for they demonstrate the prevailing internalized images. In practice, the pictures that emerge are monochromatic. They expose the failure within each parent to generate a coherent sense of the self, especially in relationship to dependency and autonomy.

Mrs. Bienegro was the last child of a poor, strict, Midwestern Catholic farming couple. She remembers often being told by her "cold, withdrawn mother" that she was an unwanted child and that there "was not enough food." Emotional supplies were also sparse: she remembers following her mother around, wishing she would smile and wondering what she had done wrong. Her reconstruction of her earlier life presents an unrelieved picture of deprivation, a picture that provides defensive justification for her subsequent repudiation of her family.

Mrs. Bienegro sees herself as having become very independent in relation to her family. She left home early in high school in order to "earn money" and insisted on paying her own college bills. She refused an allowance from her parents because "they wanted to control me." Expression of her independence required her to disavow all family values: she moved into a biracial dormitory, indulged in premarital sex, and married a man of a different religion and nationality. She remembers that when she had earlier approached her parents for what she needed, she was told, "Grow up, don't be a baby." These critical, frustrating interactions over time led to a denial of her dependency and an unconscious association of dependent needs with feelings of "badness." But, as may be seen from her rejection of what she felt was their "control," she was enraged that her dependent longings were repeatedly repulsed by her parents. She projected this anger onto her parents, whom she then treated as "hostile," thus enabling herself to leave them. But since her marriage she has felt guilty for what she "did to [her] parents." Here we have the beginnings of connection between her present perception of herself—guilt over her hostile rejection of her parents—and prevailing projections about the aggressive meanings of dependency within the Bienegro family.

Although Mr. Bienegro recalls predominantly positive images of his relationship with his family, he was also unable to get the necessary emotional sustenance. The youngest son of wealthy, elderly South Americans, Mr. Bienegro was overprotected and pampered. He was praised as long as he entertained his parents but severely punished when he transgressed. Throughout his childhood he was allowed to run up large accounts at local stores ("Money was always available," he says). He seldom, however, discussed anything with his "distant" parents.

In his early adolescence, he and a friend were caught pinching the family maid. His parents abruptly sent him off to boarding school for six months without any discussion. He saw this as typical of the many austere punishments he received at home, where "the retribution was always much heavier than the sins." In relation to his family, Mr. Bienegro saw himself as "compliant" but independent, and he recognized no anger or needfulness in response to his parents. They would not tolerate angry outbursts and reserved their marginal involvement for his "best behavior." At age sixteen, Mr. Bienegro abruptly left home for good, without a word to his parents or to his older sister, Sarah (for whom his daughter is named), who had cared for him and with whom he had spent much of his adolescence. His departure coincided with Sarah's marriage, which, he recalls, he considered "a rejection of me."

But he was unaware of any emotional response in himself. His apparent autonomy was achieved at the price of a rigid defense against any sense of his own need and depletion, which he projected onto others. After leaving home, Mr. Bienegro became an active worker for liberal causes, supporting the rights of underprivileged groups. Following his marriage, he insisted on sending money to his parents despite their relative comfort, and he now sees himself as a thoughtful, generous man.

The Bienegro marriage provided both husband and wife with a convenient partner for sustaining their particular dissociated sense of themselves. Mr. Bienegro can maintain his self-perception as "good" (warm, generous, and strong) in relation to his children because of his wife's willingness to accept his delineation of her as "bad" (cold, depriving, and fragile). She accepts this out of her own guilt and her need to see herself in a depriving relationship with her children in order to protect herself (and them) from her disavowed, aggressively tinged wishes to merge with them. In addition, by denying her own ("bad") wishes for dependent gratification, she protects her husband's fragile generosity by not making any real demands on him.

So much for background. The following two excerpts from family therapy sessions demonstrate the nature of the parental interaction. In the first excerpt, the illusion of the marriage is illustrated by Mr. Bienegro's defensive description of his wife as fragile and unable to provide, a projection necessitated by his own insecurity when he leaves the family on business trips. It is important to notice that Sarah's view of her mother corresponds to father's view and is not affected by mother's mild denials.

Excerpt I

SARAH: Well (pause), I know, Dad, whenever you go on trips and stuff like that, you sort of said, "Well, be nice to your mother, and, ah, make sure—help her out and everything," and—I used to—I don't know, Mom, I just don't think you're going to be able to handle things—if I, uh—something was to happen to Dad, you'd just go crazy. You couldn't handle the whole family, I've always had that feeling, the feeling that you'd just sort of fall apart or something—and, like, when Dad found out I was pregnant—he said, "Well, be extra nice at home because of Mom, because she's—all upset."

MOTHER: I—you know—I don't know where that comes from, I thought I was always—

FATHER: I probably am, am responsible as anybody for that.

MOTHER: You really think I'm not going to, you know—

FATHER: Well, ah—it's not that I don't think that you'll make it. I'm just worried that—ah—that the strains and stresses will get too much.

MOTHER: What's going to happen?

FATHER: I don't know (laughs), but I've never wanted to find out.

MOTHER: Well, what do you imagine—what do you imagine?

FATHER: Well, you know—sometimes you do just—get very irrational. Just (pause) so that it's—almost impossible to—

THERAPIST: What's your fear? How frightening is it that you can't say it?

FATHER: Nervous breakdown or whatever you want—to call it.

MOTHER: I don't really think you need to worry about it.

FATHER: Well, but it is something that I—have—been uneasy about.

Mr. Bienegro experiences his wife as someone who cannot "make it" without him, someone who will fall apart if left alone. In his view of their relationship, he is the autonomous adult while she is the helpless child. In addition, this description informs his children that their "bad" (fragile, "irrational") mother cannot provide for them and that they should worry about and care for her. This illusion persists despite Mrs. Bienegro's disclaimer and the reality of her competence in managing the family in his absence. As we will see in the next excerpt, Mr. Bienegro's perception represents a projection of his own fragility and inability to survive without a mothering figure.

On the rare occasions when Mrs. Bienegro leaves the home and her husband is forced to confront genuine demands, his tenuous crystalline perfection fails, and the source of the projection becomes clear:

Excerpt 2

THERAPIST: If you got up to make the kids breakfast, what would that be like for you, how would you imagine that?

FATHER: There would be all kinds of small crises to deal with and, ah, I guess, I would find them, I would find that, ah, very taxing.

THERAPIST: How do you mean?

FATHER: (Very softly) To be arguing with somebody about something and telling somebody else to do something, and a third person would find that the eggs were cooked wrong, and that would irk me as much as it does her.

MOTHER: But you're always giving me advice on how to handle things like that, Robert.

SARAH: Dad . . .

MOTHER: I really am amazed—to hear you say that kind of thing.

FATHER: Why?

MOTHER: (Loudly) Because you're always giving me advice on how to handle that kind of thing—it should not bother me—I should do it this and this way to handle it.

FATHER: Well, the fact that I give you advice doesn't mean that I'd be any more competent to handle it.

SARAH: Dad, Dad, what I think about is that time Mom went out of town and you freaked out and smashed the glass against the wall. You just couldn't handle things without Mom here, but when Mom goes away, you flip out, you don't know what to do.

FATHER: What?

SARAH: (Excitedly) You just took it up and smashed it, you know, and then started throwing stools down the stairs and breaking them. You flipped out when Mom wasn't there . . .

FATHER: I'm not denying it.

It is *Mr.* Bienegro who becomes "irrational" in the face of demands. His detached position as the warm, giving, "good" parent can be sustained only if the perception of his wife embodies this irrational aspect of his own personality. This type of transactional illusion is frequently found among authority figures in any institution.

The stability of the Bienegro marital illusion depends on the willing-ness of all members of the family to maintain these perceptions. In the absence of the "bad" mother and in the face of genuine demands, the illusion fails, and the shared parental impoverishment is revealed.

This description of the parents puts into some perspective the setting into which Sarah was born. The Bienegros can provide each other with some gratification: the husband finds this in a projected dependent self located in his wife. She in turn has her sense of impoverishment evoked and confirmed. Each of these gratifications concerns dependent wishes that they jointly perceive to be aggressive and draining demands. Sarah's birth intrudes into this balanced, if precarious, pair and disrupts it. But the disruption is more profound as her infantile demands—described by the parents as "excessive"—expose the rage the father had previously split off from himself and the rejection and disavowal of which the mother had lost sight.

Sarah was an unplanned child, and her mother concealed her preg-nancy out of embarrassment. In early childhood, Sarah had severe sepa-ration anxiety, and her father was unable to comfort her. He was often envious of her, feeling that everything revolved around her and that he did not matter. Since deprivation was a shared experience in the family, anyone in need threatened the family's equilibrium. Sarah was given drops of alcohol for her colic. Later, Sarah's temper tantrums turned into breath holding and fainting, which terrified the parents. After her sister was born, her father would come into their room at night and stifle her sister's cries with a pillow so she would not wake Sarah. He says, "From the day Sarah was born, you wouldn't cross her." Sarah remem-bers his holding her head under water to stop her crying. Neither parent felt able to provide adequately for Sarah's needs—their response was to attempt to decrease or eliminate her neediness with alcohol, avoidance, or retaliation. Terrified by being confronted with their own disavowed projections, they responded to Sarah's age-appropriate needs for nurtur-ing with anxiety, anger, and frantic attempts to constrain her.

Sarah had a relatively calm period during her early school years. In adolescence she began to socialize with inappropriate friends and asked her parents' advice about dating the son of the local Mafia head. The Bienegros again withdrew from her needs, saying, "We trust your judgment."

Unaware of her own rage and despair at her parents' lack of support, and driven by unacknowledged, intensified dependent yearnings, Sarah began to stay out all night, fail in school, and take drugs and alcohol to control her anxiety. In the two years prior to her admission to the hospital, she had been brought home stuporous from alcohol intoxication several times a week. Her alcohol use, an exaggerated re-enactment of her parents' earlier attempts to control and respond to her dependent needs with medication, was the only way in which she could allow herself to experience any neediness in relation to others. Hesitant parental questioning of her behavior evoked Sarah's rage.

Although individually distraught over Sarah's self-destructive drinking and possible promiscuity, the parents found themselves unable to confront her with it or to discuss it with each other. Although he stayed awake trembling at night awaiting Sarah's return, Mr. Bienegro avoided talking with Sarah during the day. Mrs. Bienegro could not communicate her concern to Sarah, either. Their responses reflected their defenses against parts of themselves. In order to confront their child, they would have needed to perceive, acknowledge, and internalize their own projections: Mr. Bienegro would have had to recognize his own rage as well as to admit the possibility that he was not giving his daughter the support she needed. Mrs. Bienegro would have needed to acknowledge the possibility of loving and supporting a needy child. In so doing she would have had to face her own conflicted past as a needy child and re-experience her own neediness and frustration at her own parents' unresponsiveness.

Their inability to provide assistance to Sarah—that is, to acknowledge and confront their own projections—is clarified by the following interchange. Here the parents discuss their failure to respond after finding Sarah intoxicated during a weekend pass from the hospital.

Excerpt 3

MOTHER: One way of showing you care, too, is—through a confidence, you know, in another person's judgment—you know, I think that kind of—caring—as much as always making . . .

SARAH: Well, yeah—

FATHER: (Pause) Well, every time you or Steven [brother]—or Joseph [brother]—all this is still not quite fair, but you go off somewhere, ah, we, you know, worry—or—that everything will be all right. Well, it may turn out not to be all right. But, we—cannot say "no" automatically to everything.

SARAH: Well, what do you care?

Sarah needs her parents to show their concern for her by setting limits and reacting to her self-destructiveness. What she hears is silence, and she feels abandoned. But the Bienegros unconsciously equate dependent needs with hostile demands, and thus they cannot react as she needs them to. Mr. Bienegro cannot contribute, since to confront Sarah's anger would threaten the very detachment he has adopted as his defense. He, therefore, perceives a demand that he take over *all* responsibility: "We cannot say 'no'. . . to everything." Mrs. Bienegro has similar fears. For her to provide support would reawaken her own painful longings: she rationalizes her withdrawal as "caring" by wishfully accepting Sarah's "judgment." Sarah, however, angrily recognizes that they have both failed her: "Well, what do you care?"

The isolation Sarah experienced and her experience of being lost and alone are the consequence of a family organization in which interpersonal negotiation about the meaning of individual experience within the family is not available. Without the possibility of clarifying a shared reality together, family members are left to manage by themselves. When the child who has internalized this experience of isolation within the family brings this experience into a new relationship, the cycle starts anew.

PROJECTIVE IDENTIFICATION AND AN
INTERPRETIVE FRAMEWORK

We offer this case to illuminate a key issue in our argument. The problems Sarah presents do not arise solely from within her. Nor are they the simple result of displacing the parents' pathology onto the daughter. A complex nexus of relationships is exposed and disturbed by the absence of a family structure adequate to contain anxieties at many levels—between individuals, between the couple and the children, and within the family unit itself.

Projective identification provides a way of placing an interpretive frame around the links between the individual and his context. These connections, as seen in the family of the borderline patient, illuminate a primary tension between dependency and autonomy. Many parents with borderline children remain unconsciously dependent on their own families and bring their unresolved conflicts over autonomy and dependency into their new family context. This essential conflict about the nature of dependent connections underlies the experience of being lost that we are addressing in this book. The denial of any autonomy produces a destructively dependent stance, which inhibits creative work and exploits the capacities of others. But the denial of dependency leaves the individual without the experience of connectedness. This absence of connectedness both damages the individual and interferes with the creative links between different perspectives, depleting the richness of human structures. We see this sense of isolation in families, parents, and children. But it can also be seen in the social structures and problems of our age. How this absence of connectedness develops will become clearer as we examine the sustaining forces within a group—in this case, still the family—and explore how they generate the contexts in which individuals exist.

3 ○ Containing

Chaotic Experience

The period of adolescence is a time of major and often chaotic role change. The child is moving toward adulthood, and the parents are undergoing shifts in their role relationships with the child and hence with each other as well. Because many of the overt changes, in body shape and emotional makeup, occur in the adolescent, he or she almost inevitably becomes the presenter of family pathology. The adolescent's efforts to form new relationships outside the family threaten the integrity of the boundaries of the family unit by opening it to outside scrutiny.

Each of the key sustaining elements in the family as a group—boundaries, task, and roles—is in flux. This occurs in every family, whether it produces a borderline adolescent or not. The usual, and generally reliable, supports that enable people to manage new dependent needs—for example, the comfortable reliance on a stable recognition by others of who one is—become unexpectedly unstable revealing the underlying need for the family to manage its emotional environment in new ways.

THE HOLDING ENVIRONMENT

The "holding environment" was initially described by Donald W. Winnicott (1960b). He studied the nature of the bond between mother and child, focusing on the creation of an environment that would promote basic human development. This environment has two fundamental characteristics: empathic interpretation and the tolerance and containment of aggression and sexuality. An empathic context affirms the child's sense of himself as "good." "Good" is not meant in a moral sense; instead, it describes self-affirmation, the child's sense that he is understandable, that he can be known, know himself, and have meaningful human contact with others. Parental tolerance and containment of the child's aggression and sexuality allow the child to discover that his impulses and actions motivated by them do not have to be destructive. They can be mobilized to serve a task (in this case, development) without inevitably disrupting human relationships.

The use of the term *environment* itself directs us to think of the family as an open system. The family is not simply a collection of individuals that functions in isolation. We see it instead as an organization that interacts with the external world through its various members and their liaisons. For a small child, the parents stand between the child and his world, providing links for the child through their help with communication, through their tolerance, and through their interpretation of his feelings. It is in this dimension of the family's life—the world of increasingly understandable, manageable, and interpretable feelings—that human development takes place. When this holding environment decays or is absent, as in borderline cases, the child feels unsafe in the world and is forced into premature maturation, developing what Modell (1975) calls an "illusion of self-sufficiency." In some cases, this illusory self-sufficiency appears as detachment; in others, it is revealed through the denial of dependency combined with a chaotic and seemingly unrelated series of outbursts that demand a containing response.

Failures in the holding environment during the adolescence of a particular child are not simply the result of the various pathologies of individuals within the family. Each contributes to but also joins a shared family regression, which damages and frequently destroys either or both facets of the holding environment.

Regression is a defense common to all of us. At times of stress, when our mature capacities cannot manage, we all have the capacity to shift back toward the use of psychological mechanisms more appropriate to earlier periods of our lives. Regression may entail a shift from words as communication to action or from organized imagery toward the fantastic images and simple metaphors more characteristic of a child. Or, we may alter our entire mode of relationship, from rational, organized perception toward primitive distortion and dependent clinging. In groups and families, a shared regression may evoke earlier modes of communication, loss of individual boundaries, and shared, sometimes psychotic, defenses.

Failures of empathy are often due to a regressed confusion about who the other person is. Images recalled from earlier circumstances so dominate the interactions that it becomes impossible to distinguish and locate feelings accurately. All concerned, not just the child, doubt their worth. The second aspect of holding, the containment of aggression and sexuality, also fails when boundaries between people become so blurred that they cannot be clarified and explored. In the absence of clear interpersonal boundaries, it becomes impossible to determine whose impulses are being experienced; the distinction between "the container and the contained" (Bion 1961) is lost. Family members may become confused about the family's identity when in conflict with aspects of the external world. For instance, if a young woman marries outside her family's religion, the parents may become so overwhelmed with embarrassment, confusion, and rage that they disavow their connection to her. When overcome with such struggles, the family group may encompass so much unmanageable emotion that it is not only unsure of its own definition but also uncertain whether it has a task at all.

Recognizing the existence of boundaries is a developmental achievement that, as we previously noted, arises out of the mother-child relationship. Once the mother communicates that she is affected but not destroyed by the child's impulses, the child can begin to become his own container for aggression and sexuality—that is, to become responsible for his own feelings. The discovery of individual boundaries, therefore, is crucial for development.

But simultaneously the child begins to attend to group boundaries of similar importance. The young child's parents provide the external family boundary. This boundary is not just a protective one designed to secure the family from intrusion. It is also an identity boundary comparable to the personal boundary of the young child. The development of individual and family boundaries allows sufficient self-identification to be able to negotiate—with others within the family and with the family's external world.

The family is an organization for the management of social experience. It has, therefore, a number of related tasks and individuals in different roles. These qualities relate the family to organizations in general. The themes of task and role will occupy us for much of the rest of the book. First, however, we offer an outline of these two issues specifically in relation to the family.

TASK AND ROLE IN THE FAMILY

Task refers to the reason for the family's existence. Individuals, who will participate in many other groups throughout their lives, discover in the family a paradigm of shared behavior. The realization that it is possible to recognize and value the separateness of individuals (including oneself) and still join others in a task begins in the family. With such conscious joining, both connectedness and separateness can be acknowledged.

Role is a more complex notion. In a family the usual roles are father, mother, son, daughter, brother, sister, and so forth. These terms not only stand for kinship names but can also be viewed as roles—aspects of the family's task. So, for example, parental roles do not just designate relationships, and they are more complex in terms of gender identifications, muscular body interactions, and the like than the economic or other stereotyped roles such as breadwinner, disciplinarian, nurturer, or housekeeper. The roles of "father" and "mother" also comprise aspects of the larger shared family task of promoting development.

In these family roles, individuals experience themselves as individuals, but their personal behavior is restricted by their roles. For example, parents can experience feelings of competition or sexual attraction toward younger men or women. But because of their parental roles they exercise constraints on themselves when exploring these feelings in relation to their children.

Whatever effect roles may have on individual behavior in relationships, they do not originate with the individual. All the roles in a family derive from there being a family in the first place. And the complex entity that is a family is not composed of a random set of relationships. The family is a distinctive unit defined by its task to contribute to the development of its members. In furtherance of that task, the family defines its boundaries and roles and negotiates with the external world. We therefore see roles as contingent upon the task. When a family loses sight of its task or adopts an inappropriate task, the consequent role confusion for each member produces pathological symptoms in individuals and degeneracy in the family unit.

However, unconscious conflicts and shared fantasies within families can create a further series of roles. These we may describe as "irrational roles," for example, the "good father" or the "rebellious teenager" are roles that irrationally exclude complexity and ambivalence in the service of unconscious needs. But irrational roles are not insignificant, nor are they always evidence of disturbance. They may have a key function as elements of a transitory, but necessary and task-related, family dynamic. For example, the irrational creation of a "good father" through the network of projective identification pervading a family may ultimately need to be disentangled and interpreted if developmental tasks are to be pursued satisfactorily. But it may also contribute significantly and usefully to the holding environment that is needed. The "good father" may be an important idealizing experience for a boy at the beginning of his gender role development. Irrational roles may also help to assure members of a family that their individual and familial irrationalities are not unaddressable or merely delinquent.

We may now link these ideas of task and role with the concept of the holding environment and its functions of containing impulses and providing accurate empathic interpretation. The basic structures of the holding environment are task, boundaries, and role. Within these structures, containment of impulses and interpretation take place through acknowledging individuality (curiosity), bearing painful affect (containment), and putting in perspective (empathic interpretation in context).[1] The containing and interpreting that occurs within the holding environment provides individuals with the opportunity to become aware of their projections and to reinternalize them. Through so doing they achieve a more complex sense of themselves, a more empathic view of others, and a strengthened ability to join with others in different roles in a shared task. In other words, they grow and develop.

ILLUSTRATION: THE HOLDING ENVIRONMENT IN THE BIENEGRO FAMILY

To clarify how the holding environment functions, we present an example of difficulties that occurred within the Bienegro family's holding environment and how these were addressed in family therapy.[2] Each of the following four excerpts represents a step in the process by which the family unit rediscovers its task.

Excerpt 1: Failure of the Holding Environment
Sarah is discussing an unusual attempt on her part to talk with her father about feeling depressed. The family appears to unite in a powerful statement that the adolescent could not have expressed such needs

and that the father, the giving, "loving" parent, could not have ignored her.

SARAH: (To father) You said something to me and I said that I was depressed. And you said, "Why don't you go to sleep—maybe you'll feel better." And I said, "No, Dad, I don't think sleeping will help," and then you just walked out.

THERAPIST: You wanted some other response?

SARAH: I suppose—suppose I wanted to talk—about it.

FATHER: And I walked away?

SARAH: Yeah.

THERAPIST: You don't remember this incident?

FATHER: (Pause) I remember—that "I am depressed"—yeah. But I certainly don't . . . (long pause).

THERAPIST: And how do you remember your response?

FATHER: (Pause) I remember some—vague—ah—obviously unsuccessful attempt to—I—find out what it was about.

SARAH: (Softly) No, Dad, your reaction was that I should go to sleep.

FATHER: (Pause) I can't believe, Sarah, if you tell me that you were depressed—I find it almost impossible to believe that I would have done that—Saturday night.

THERAPIST: (To mother) Do *you* believe it?

MOTHER: What? . . . (low voice) I don't know.

SARAH: Look, I'm saying that this is what happened. Don't you believe me?

MOTHER: You're saying that, he says it didn't—I didn't hear—(to the therapist) I'm surprised to hear that Sarah would come out and say that she was depressed.

THERAPIST: Me, too. But do you believe her?

MOTHER: (Pause, low voice) I don't really know.

THERAPIST: (To brothers) Do you believe her?

STEVEN: (Pause) I don't know.

JOSEPH: No.

MOTHER: I guess he *could* have said it, but then again he wouldn't necessarily have said it.

FATHER: (Pause) I wish I could be a—because I can honestly not believe it, Sarah. I—I'm sure that it happened—in some fashion —and that you heard it that way. I'm also sure that I didn't *say* it that way. You know?

THERAPIST: Why are you so sure?

FATHER: Because I would *not*! I just would *not*!

THERAPIST: You have a tendency, you have said, not to see painful things.

FATHER: I also have—uh—have fought the tendency very hard. I realize it sounds weaselly, but—ah—there was—there *had* to be—in between "I am depressed" and "Why don't you,"—I mean—I can believe that both statements were said . . .

SARAH: (Shouting) You didn't even ask me what it was about, Dad! You did not!

Family members cannot acknowledge that Sarah might have turned to father and been rejected. Though we cannot know what actually happened, what is of interest here is the images that family members have in their minds of one another and the degree of certainty with which they hold those images. The powerful shared repudiation of Sarah represents each family member's projection onto her of their own neediness. They each anxiously protect father as a representation of their own wishes to be generous and responsive. Given this shared defensive fantasy about father, which denies his fragility, Sarah's desire to discuss her depression is unconsciously experienced as a hostile, draining demand on meager resources. The other members of the family unite for their own protection to deny the possibility of such behavior.

Such intense defensive projection from the group results in an impairment of Sarah's sense of reality. She is faced with an impossible dilemma. She can either hold onto her own perception of reality and be estranged from the family, or she can capitulate to them (saying, "O.K., it never happened") and surrender her differentiation and her sense of reality.

This is an appalling personal dilemma for Sarah. But behind this level of confusion is another serious loss, that has repercussions for all concerned—the loss of the family's task. Without the context of the task, through which the range of developmental tasks is facilitated, Sarah may not develop her inhibited capacities for separation and individuation; Mr. and Mrs. Bienegro may not integrate themselves personally as they attempt to take up their parental roles; and the boys, with Sarah, may not discover their sibling roles. The overall developmental task of the family, which would generate a variety of facilitating roles, is collusively replaced by the shared defensive task of avoiding anxiety and preserving inflexible roles.

Excerpt 2: Reassurance

In the second excerpt, two months later, the family continues its exploration of their shared fantasy that neediness and depression are intolerable. It opens with another example of the father's difficulty in listening to his daughter's sense of helplessness.

SARAH: Well, I can't see too much in the future for me—most of the time.

FATHER: Well, that usually puts an end to the conversation and it's very hard to—

SARAH: (Angrily) Well, what can I say when that's the way it is, you know—where am I going? I mainly think in terms of, uh, just taking off again and maybe something—somewhere I'll find—you know—something good will happen around here. What kind of job can I get? Work some shitty job all my life?

FATHER: You're not a moron, you have at least normal capabilities so that you don't have to stay in one job. Your saying that you see nothing in the future doesn't make sense to me.

THERAPIST: Pessimism, apparently, is a difficult thing to share.

FATHER: I can share her feeling of not knowing what to do—where I don't go along is where she translates "I don't know what to do" into "I can't do anything" because that's not true.

THERAPIST: That's not what she said either. At least, that's not what I heard. I heard, "I see nothing in my future"—and you've often thought that about her, too.

FATHER: Yes, unless she decides to *do* something.

The excerpt illustrates how Sarah's father continually tries to "cheer her up." This fruitless attempt not only alienates her from him but represents his effort to save himself from his own despair, which he has projected. In this kind of boundary blurring, individuals cannot perceive which of their needs belong to them and which are being projected. Such boundary blurring is especially characteristic of a group in regression, for the boundaries are often blurred for the group as a whole, not just for a single individual. Thus by focusing on the group, and especially on the boundary that defines that group and its task, the therapist is able to make a significantly clarifying intervention. This intervention derives from the premise that no one in the group is "nonactive." When a member is silent, that silence is significant. In this case, one hypothesis is that silence represents covert support for the person speaking. Noticing that the other members of the family have remained silent, the therapist suggests in the following interchange that the father speaks for the family. In so doing he publicly identifies the irrational *role* the father has adopted, differentiating it implicitly from the *person* the father is. Identifying this role indirectly suggests to the father that he might have some conscious control over what role he takes up and that he might choose otherwise. This is the first step (acknowledgement) in reconstructing the holding environment.

THERAPIST: See, my perception is that when you're all feeling that way, you can't talk about it—unless someone is feeling the other way. (To father) You generally represent the hopeful voice in the family.

SARAH: (Mimicking father) "You look fine from the outside, perfectly fine—nothing looks wrong."

THERAPIST: You don't find that reassuring?

SARAH: No!

THERAPIST: (To father) I wonder why you're content in accepting the role in the family as the one who's always optimistic.

FATHER: Well, my immediate reply is somebody's got to.

Here, the father perceives the role clarification and begins to think in terms of the family as a group. Sarah, surprisingly, agrees.

SARAH: That was mine, too.

THERAPIST: Why?

The father's next response incorporates the therapist's notion of roles and advances the interpretive work by offering an interpretation about the shared unconscious fantasy that is interfering with task definition and disrupting the holding environment.

FATHER: The—the whole family—sinks into the swamp of despair.

THERAPIST: And depression is dangerous—somebody has to hold the family above the swamp?

MOTHER: Well, the fact of the matter is that it doesn't work (laughs).

THERAPIST: That's right—(to father) it doesn't even work for you.

As the therapist continues to clarify the shared sense that depression is intolerable, the polarization between Sarah and her father (gloomy versus optimistic) decreases. Sarah begins to reveal her ambivalent response to her father's optimism: she both scorns it ("nothing looks wrong") and supports it ("that was mine, too"). When mother observes that the forced optimism "doesn't work," father and Sarah begin to acknowledge a shared sadness.

> SARAH: This is so depressing. I had a good day at work today, and now I just feel really shitty.
>
> FATHER: Well, I don't know, but ah—somehow to have a—a gathering of people, forever looking at the horizon and seeing a little cloud and talking about the *rain* that's going to fall sometime, it just is awfully depressing—you just, you know—so if no one else is going to do anything about it, I'll just keep trying because it gets to be pretty oppressive (tears in eyes).
>
> THERAPIST: And you feel like you can't stand it?
>
> FATHER: That's right.
>
> THERAPIST: I think that feeling is worth examining. It's in all of you. The notion that depression is intolerable—and to acknowledge it would destroy you in some way.
>
> MOTHER: It isn't pleasant. I guess I'm afraid it's contagious.

With this comment, the mother has joined in the thinking about a shared family fantasy, taking it a step further by linking the idea of intolerable depression to that of a contagious disease. This notion makes it clear why any member of this family who acknowledges sadness is ostracized and kept in a kind of psychological isolation room. Whoever becomes the bearer of sadness also becomes a container for unwanted family projections.

> THERAPIST: As long as Mr. Bienegro remains cheerful, you know he hasn't caught it (Mrs. Bienegro laughs). (To father) It's not very hard, though, to see the tears behind your cheerfulness.
>
> FATHER: Occasionally, yes (clears throat). (Sarah gets up to leave).

As father moves out of the position of "optimist" and notices his own depression, Sarah becomes anxious.

> SARAH: I don't want to be here. Things were beginning to look up and this is really depressing and I don't want to be here.
>
> THERAPIST: So when your father's not taking the role of being cheery, you feel some pressure to do it—for the family—to find some way to escape.
>
> SARAH: Uh huh.

This excerpt particularly demonstrates that pressures to maintain a shared fantasy belong to the group as a whole, not to individuals. The assumption appears to be that depression—here, the experience of hopelessness—is intolerable. Other members of the family protect themselves by localizing these feelings in Sarah and repudiating her. As these assumptions are clarified and made conscious, each projection is progressively withdrawn. The shared neediness and depletion in the family are exposed. The interpretive approach based upon the primacy of the group offers the family the recognition that anxiety and neediness are shared and that individuals can be responsible for their own neediness without producing guilt and withdrawal in others.

Excerpt 3: Boundary Formation

Sarah, after repeatedly telling her parents she would like them to kick her out of the house, has come home drunk and riotous. Father, for the first time, has asked her to leave. This action is out of character with his previous "all-giving" father role. It indicates his painful acceptance of a boundary between himself and his daughter and a recognition that he is not responsible for and cannot fulfill all of his daughter's needs. He must, therefore, begin to examine his own needs. This action represents a reinternalization of a previously disavowed, needy aspect of himself and leaves him filled with a new experience of sadness.

FATHER: Well, I uh—(sighs)—Friday night I spent most of the night dreaming about Sarah being dead, which was kind of ghastly. And, uh—and then after we talked Saturday and after I took her out to her apartment, I—I—I had (pause) I just felt (pause) like a—inside, like a broken spring or something and I never could quite define why or—or what had happened. (Softly, slowly, hesitantly) Obviously, it was, uh—it was connected with talking with Sarah about her staying at home, and also (sigh) I kind of felt that I—she was kind of drowning and—I, I just walked away without trying to do anything about it—and the combination of the two was quite—rather unpleasant. Then, uh, last night all at once it seemed like perhaps what had happened was—I don't know whether that's sound or not but at the time it seemed at least that somehow I'd cut an apron string or something and—and, just—Sarah was there and I was here and, uh, I wasn't altogether wrapped up and I could maintain some kind of distance which I didn't feel I could before (pause).

THERAPIST: (To Sarah) What's your reaction to this?

SARAH: I don't know, I was thinking, how glad I am to be out of the house, you know, I feel so much better.

THERAPIST: Well, what about what your father was saying?

SARAH: I was falling apart living there too.

THERAPIST: Seems to me that people in the family have a hard time acknowledging how badly they feel when someone important has left them (pause).

At this point, family members become aware of a new aspect of father, who had not previously acknowledged his own sadness. In fact, when father initially gave his own history, he reported that his adolescence was wonderful and free from any emotional conflict. As he reinternalizes the intolerable sadness previously projected onto his nineteen-year-old daughter, he is able to put an element of his own adolescence in perspective.

MOTHER: I don't know, it's funny, you know, the difference in reaction. Usually it's I who gets down and rolls and cries and so on and I've never really seen Joe like this before. I mean, he was so, you know, wow. I never really saw it. I felt sad and, but somehow I, uh, managed—well, my explanation of it is that obviously, it touched something in him which it didn't touch in me—it may or may not be different experiences or something. Then we were trying to figure out, you know, what it was, and why it should be. And—and obviously it has, I don't know, seems to me something to do with his separation, you know. He's always said that when he left home that really he was all right, you know. He never . . .

FATHER: Well, I was extremely sad all the time.

THERAPIST: What was that like? I've not heard from you much about your feelings.

FATHER: It was very hard, because I had to tell everybody goodbye without, uh—as if I were just leaving for the afternoon. Of course, I had no idea when I'd ever come back. Except for my brother, I told him. But it was very—extremely hard.

THERAPIST: And you were how old?

FATHER: Nineteen.

THERAPIST: What do you remember?

FATHER: I remember going to go get a train and going into my friend's house and flopping down and just—as a matter of fact the same as I was when (to mother) you came into the room the other night—flopping down and just crying my heart out.

THERAPIST: (To mother) You were saying that this was a new thing to you, to realize how strongly he could feel about separation.

MOTHER: I guess so because I've honestly never seen him so sad, you know.

Through this phase, aspects of the holding environment—which have hitherto been so obscure that they have been lost—have been restored. Roles have been clarified, feelings have been acknowledged, tolerated, interpreted, and put in perspective. Projections have been reinternalized, boundaries strengthened, and relationships changed.

Excerpt 4: Resolution

Two months later, in a family therapy session, the father realizes with some surprise that his daughter no longer scares him. As he investigates this change, he describes the altered experience of his relationship with his daughter.

FATHER: I was thinking that, uh, Sarah doesn't really scare me anymore. I'm scared by *things*, but Sarah herself doesn't . . .

THERAPIST: What's changed?

FATHER: I don't really know—ah, I—I think that the critical time came about two months or so ago, and I kind of—I don't think she became distant—I don't think she's distant at all, but uh I kind of saw her as—as "she was there and I was here" and that was it. And uh—

SARAH: You mean when I left—you mean after the thing at home —when I—I kind of came out of the dumps after that.

THERAPIST: You felt that way too, Sarah—something had changed?

SARAH: Yeah. I felt something was changed since then.

THERAPIST: Can you describe it?

SARAH: (Pause) They still affect me, but you know, I feel I can come and go and—I don't know—just . . . (pause)

FATHER: I think, for instance, last Thursday I was very worried about whether you were all right, whether you had gotten drunk and passed out, and uh then Mary told me what happened, and I still had some slight, uh, definite uncertainty as to the exact facts, but at least it seemed as if you were all right.

SARAH: Well, what—what are you saying, that just because I stopped drinking like I was, is that why you're not—

FATHER: No, no, no that has nothing—that probably is bound in with it, but that's not the basic fact. No. I'm saying that I'm not as—I'm still very concerned about you and what you do, but uh I can uh, I'm not so totally quiveringly connected, you know, that anything that happens I'm just a bowl of jelly ah and therefore I can uh—I'm not destroyed by everything that happens. I'm thinking of just my own side.

THERAPIST: Is it fair to say that you see yourself as a separate person more—

FATHER: Well, that's what I'm trying to say, yeah. That I'm here and she's there. I worry about her but I'm not—you know, if uh—if your friend had told me that uh you got drunk, I would have been very sorry about it and possibly, probably mad at you for doing it, but I wouldn't have gotten just totally destroyed, I don't think.

SARAH: Well, I think now that I feel like I have the right—like I can come and go, like going to the country and stuff, but—and not feeling guilty about a lot of things, like before, feeling like I had to explain everything—I don't know.

FATHER: For instance, I think that uh last year, I would have been rather shattered if you had gone off to the country on my birthday, and—it didn't . . .

SARAH: Well, I felt a little bad about it, but it didn't—I thought, well—

FATHER: Well, that's right, you should feel a little bad, but it's . . . and I—didn't feel any—either neglected or—

SARAH: Yeah, I was wondering if you had.

FATHER: No, I didn't.

An empathic respect for each other's experience is tentatively developing in father and daughter. As contrasted with Excerpt 1, where the relationship was characterized by alienation and confusion, this interaction reveals a more supportive, complex, and flexible interchange in which ambivalent responses can coexist and be understood.

Were we to follow this through, we should arrive at a clearer perception, too, of the boundary around the Bienegro family. The clarification of the relationship between father and daughter derives from a shared recognition in the family that the task of facilitating individual development (here chiefly Sarah's) is primary. This increasing clarity about task encourages assurance about roles—in particular the roles of father and daughter.

Painful and aggressive feelings have been acknowledged, borne, and interpreted in relation to their appropriate contexts. As a consequence, the opportunity exists for more creative, less stereotyped interaction between family members; previously experienced despair and hopelessness about shared endeavor have disappeared. This is a central aspect of the holding environment, here recreated by the family with interpretive clarification of boundaries provided by the therapist.

The story of the Bienegro family illustrates the crucial importance of a holding environment. Its absence during Sarah's early years (and during her parents' early years as well) prevented her from developing secure boundaries within herself as an individual and within her family unit as a whole. The need for a holding environment, however, is not confined to a specific stage in child development. Accurate empathy and containment of impulses remain crucial for any human interaction.

During therapy a new holding environment was constructed, but not in order to compensate for its absence during the previous seventeen years. We are not suggesting that, given the right conditions, the past can somehow be corrected. Instead, Sarah, and to some degree other members of her family, was able to address some of the consequences of that initial deprivation as these consequences became evident in her present experience of herself and of her parents. As we shall later demonstrate, however, this task is not merely a task for therapy. The holding environment, designed to provide empathic acknowledgment, containment, and perspective, forms a crucial dimension of all organizational and institutional life. Its loss in any context constitutes a serious deprivation and may contribute more to individual disturbance and to institutional irrationality and organizational disarray than has hitherto been recognized.

4 ○ Interpreting

from Within

Given the complexity and passion of family interactions, it is not surprising that when therapists first begin working with disturbed families, they are initially confused. This confusion has two primary sources. First, much of the data about family interaction is not presented in words. Second, in addition to observing what is going on within the family unit from the outside, therapists become aspects of that unit by interacting with others. As they do so, they begin to absorb the dynamics of the family system and experience them within themselves. This is the "participant" aspect of the participant-observer method, so central to the development of a negotiated interpretive stance. Here we will look at what this participation entails and what it contributes to the development of a holding environment.

THE HOLDING ENVIRONMENT AND THE
THERAPIST'S PERSPECTIVE

As we have seen in the Bienegro case, members of a disturbed family have difficulty recognizing the nature of their individual and shared irrationality because they are immersed in it. The pressures on therapists simply to join the family system with all its well-established irrationality are enormous. Therapists must often undergo a kind of regression within themselves in order to discover the connections between their own experiences and those of the family. But this regression is not merely a facet of the therapeutic environment. As we shall show, the capacity to regress in the interest of learning is an essential component of the ability to locate oneself in a series of contexts in a turbulent world.

In the first set of excerpts that follow, note that the therapist unwittingly repeats pathological aspects of the Bienegro family's failed holding environment in his individual therapy with the patient.[1] He is able to grasp this repetition because he has witnessed the dynamics of the family as a unit.

Excerpt 1

Earlier we saw that when Sarah recalled her efforts to discuss her depression with her father her family reacted with disbelief. The family united in trying to tell her that such a thing could not possibly have happened and that she must have imagined it. Their shared denial left Sarah lost, confused, angry, and doubting her perception of reality.

In her individual therapy session later that afternoon, Sarah began by discussing her anger with "the rigid staff rules" under which "nobody [was] allowed to see [her]." In fact, the staff had limited her visitors and required them to check in because several had brought drugs on previous visits. In reading the following excerpt, it is important to keep in mind Sarah's hurt and angry response in the earlier family session, when family members suggested that what she perceived was not so. Sarah's opening statement—"Nobody is allowed to see me"—is an unconscious expression of her need to talk to the therapist, a need that is parallel to her attempt to discuss her depression with her father. The therapist does not at first perceive this parallel need and responds only to the apparent content. Sarah's angry response is immediate, uncontrollable, and seemingly inappropriate.

SARAH: Nobody is allowed to see me!

THERAPIST: That is something of a distortion, that visitors are *not allowed* to see you.

SARAH: Joe [a friend] had to talk to a staff member.

THERAPIST: That doesn't mean he's not allowed to see you.

SARAH: Fred [a friend] was kicked off the unit.

THERAPIST: You say that in a tone . . .

SARAH: (Shouting) Oh, fuck you!

THERAPIST: . . . that indicates that it's an arbitrary staff that would just kick Fred off the unit for no reason at all.

SARAH: (Softly) Of course there's some reason.

THERAPIST: You were hurt when I said that. What are you angry about?

SARAH: (Long pause, then angrily) "It's a distortion," just like every-
thing I say is a distortion.
THERAPIST: Everything you say is *not* a distortion.
(Sarah, swearing, runs angrily from the room, slamming the door.)

The therapist did not recognize Sarah's opening statement as an unconscious reference to her family in which nobody is "allowed" to see her *as
she is* because of the family's defensive structure. Guilty about setting
limits on Sarah, he responded defensively and concretely to her anger,
unwittingly replicating the family's reaction by suggesting that she was
distorting reality.[2] The experience with the family was so powerful and
the parallel to it so close that Sarah momentarily lost the distinction
between therapist and father. Her internal sense of being unacknowledged by her father suddenly matched her experience with the therapist.
Overwhelmed by pain and rage, Sarah fled from the room leaving the
therapist feeling lost in a familiar place, without guideposts, since he did
not recognize that Sarah was responding to him.

Excerpt 2
When Sarah returned ten minutes later, her rage was unabated.

(Sarah reenters, slamming the door)
SARAH: (Angrily) I'm not going to let you fuck up my passes[3]—I
don't have anything else to say to you. I want to go out with Joe this
weekend, so I came back.
THERAPIST: I don't know why you left.
SARAH: (Tearfully) Because I'm sick of hearing my "distortions
of the truth," and that I "lie," you know? Because it *is* the truth.
There may be other things, you know, but they're *not* allowed on
the unit for various reasons. It may be my fault, but it's still the
truth, and I—I told them why they weren't allowed on, it's not like
I said it was other people's fault, you know. (Crying) I said it was
my fault.

Sarah's tearful response to a gentle attempt to examine her behavior
allowed the therapist, who had initially experienced her rage as bewil-
deringly inappropriate, to recognize her appeal. In addition, her acceptance of her own responsibility ("I said it was my fault") relieved the
therapist of some of his excessive guilt, contributing to the shared holding environment for the therapeutic work. With this the therapist found
himself in a more familiar place and could recognize the repetition of
the earlier family dynamic in the current relationship. As he and Sarah

explore the repetition, Sarah graphically describes her experience of being lost in a familiar place — in a family organization where people relate to their projections and not to her.

Excerpt 3

THERAPIST: You thought I was saying to you what your father said to you this morning.

SARAH: (Shouting) Yes!

THERAPIST: (Pause) I can see why you ran out.

SARAH: (Tearfully) You just sit there laughing, "distortion of the truth," you know. It's real funny.

THERAPIST: I understand now why you were so hurt. (Pause) I'm glad you came back.

SARAH: (Tearfully) I didn't want to come back, you know, at all. But I'd just be fucking myself over and I've done enough of that, you know.

THERAPIST: That was confusing for you this morning when nobody believed you.

SARAH: (Tearfully) Yeah, it was, I was just flipping out, you know! Like maybe I didn't hear it [i.e., her father's telling her to go to bed], but I *know I did*! (Crying)

THERAPIST: I believe you. (Long pause) In fact, that was the first time that I understood what you meant about things being very strange — spaced out — because I felt that you were being extruded by everyone in the family.

SARAH: Afterwards, my mother said she believed me, you know? (Pause) That's how it is in my family, everyone just floats around all the time — gotta pretend everything's fine.

THERAPIST: And when you know that it isn't, it makes you feel crazy?

SARAH: After a while, I don't know any more — in thinking back — I just thought it was all in my head, you know. I really didn't even know if it's just me, or what! (Crying) I just didn't know! You know, it's sort of like when I first started getting spaced out and I didn't understand what was going on. It was like — people were talking — would talk to me and I didn't know whether they were talking to me or somebody else, even if they were looking right at me.

THERAPIST: Well, that's what was happening this morning in family therapy. Did you have that same feeling when I said that what you said was a distortion?

SARAH: You said it sort of laughingly, you know, like—like I was saying things crazy or something, like I didn't know what I was talking about. Just that word stuck in my mind, you know, like I can see now what you were saying. It was just the way it hit me . . .

The therapist employed several interventions, including rapid and concrete interpretation of Sarah's angry reaction ("You thought I was saying to you what your father said"), clarification of reality ("you . . . were being extruded"), and support for her appropriate dependent needs ("I'm glad you came back"). This containment of her aggression combined with an empathic interpretation allowed the holding environment to be reestablished for Sarah as her return had reestablished it for the therapist. Once back in a shared holding environment, Sarah could continue her own interpretive work on the psychological sources of her behavior and feelings by using her capacities to observe the family ("gotta pretend everything's fine") and understand herself and her work with the therapist ("I can see now what you were saying").

This mutual learning derived from a shared regression between therapist and patient that resulted in Sarah's flight from the room. Although the therapist, in his defensive remark ("That's something of a distortion") was insufficiently perceptive and affected by his own guilty feelings about limiting her privileges, Sarah's anger was excessive. Because she was projecting her own aggressiveness, she experienced the therapist's defensive comment as an assault. Despite the therapist's momentary loss of himself and his role in his failure to provide either containment or empathy for his patient, he and she together were able to recover the holding environment and learn from its inadequacy.

This phenomenon furthers our thinking on the dynamic nature of the holding environment. "Holding" may seem to represent an ideal—stable and consistent. But it is in fact a much more fluid context, characterized by the way in which its failures can be used for learning. By sharing her painful experience with her family and recognizing its repetition in the individual therapeutic relationship, Sarah was able to use the therapist's observations to confirm her sense of reality about her family role and to find herself again. This was an important step for Sarah. In our subsequent discussions about individuals and their orientation within organizations in general we will have more to say about the benefits to be derived from the participant-observer stance. Joining a system in a distinctive role offers the possibility of being both immersed in the role and yet sufficiently distant to observe. Recovery of this perspective is crucial if any interpretive work is to be done, whether by a therapist with a patient or by any person who is lost in any familiar place.

IMMERSION AND PERSPECTIVE—THE BROWN FAMILY

The case illustrations so far have concerned a single family and their interactions with one another and, to some extent, the therapist. The following story focuses explicitly on the therapist and the way in which he uses his own experience to identify and contain the most difficult aspects of the family's disturbance. What this illustrates is the process of collaboratively developing a holding environment. The therapist's immersion in the family system is more than momentary, since the effects of the powerful dynamics of the family remain with him and enter his private life. Using the framework we have outlined, the therapist focuses on boundaries, roles, and tasks. As he does so, he becomes filled with painful experiences in relation to his task, which he then offers to the family to consider.

The Brown family consists of Mr. and Mrs. Brown and their three adolescent sons, including Fred, a profoundly isolated sixteen-year-old boy. Fred was hospitalized after a series of suicide attempts, most recently by hanging. Two therapists were assigned to the family treatment. One met with the boy, the other with the parents, and both therapists together with the entire family group.

The family interaction was characterized by obliqueness, indirectness, a suspicious, detached stance on the part of the adolescent, and a profound sense of helplessness and incompetence on the part of the parents. They clearly wanted the two therapists to take over and tell them both how they had failed as parents and what to do to change the situation. Communication within the family appeared to be carried out largely through behavior rather than words, and feelings were not easily recognized or discussed.

Over the course of a lengthy period in the hospital, Fred became less self-destructive. But he and his family continued to have difficulty establishing a working alliance with the therapists that would allow the tension-filled interactions within the family and between family members and treatment staff to be addressed and interpreted. In the central family triangle, mother, father, and Fred adopted stereotyped positions: mother was guilt-laden, weepy, and ineffectual; father was brusque, insensitive, and preoccupied with his work; Fred remained aloof, unconnected, and sullen. The Browns responded to Fred with great delicacy and hesitation, experiencing him as fragile, incomprehensible, unpredictable, and alien. In part, this defensive parental withdrawal and fear of Fred were determined by how much they had suffered from his current anger, suicidal withdrawal, and hatred; in part, it represented the outcome of chronic difficulties in family members' capacities to communicate feelings verbally.

After Fred had improved enough to be transferred to a halfway house[4] towards the end of the first year of therapy, the parents' repeated cancellations and frequent rescheduling of weekly family therapy sessions became increasingly confusing for the therapists. At random times during the therapy session, the parents would propose a new time for the next meeting and occasionally during the week they would phone in to reschedule again. The therapists' struggles to focus on the task of therapy seemed to be of no avail. Attempts to connect the cancellations with events in the sessions themselves were fruitless. Father, whose successful business life required frequent trips, became instantly suspicious when his plans were questioned; he seemed to be unaware that his absences had an impact on family members. Mother, who joined him on many of these trips, seemed passive and confused. None of the children had any comments about the cancellations and seemed indifferent. Fred remained detached and participated only in a superficial, sarcastic manner, often remaining silent.

In his individual therapy, Fred developed an intensely negative reaction to the therapist, whom he viewed as powerful, controlling, and fearsome. He was unable to accept any ideas from the therapist or to tell the therapist when he was in distress. At the same time, his pattern of attendance at individual therapy sessions became increasingly irregular. He would come late, "forget" the time, arrange another meeting during the hour, or remain silent. In general, he demonstrated his sense of not feeling in a reliable holding environment and his inability to develop a predictable relationship with his therapist.

The therapist, who had initially been able to engage Fred individually around a discussion of anger, began to feel disconnected; the therapy was in a stalemate. Together both therapists felt hopeless, confused, and unable to think clearly about the treatment. They wondered whether Fred should be returned to the hospital and struggled with the possibility that the family could simply not be engaged. Some link seemed to exist between the adolescent's behavior and that of his parents, but all relationships seemed disconnected and unfocused. The therapists speculated that their feelings of helplessness and the discontinuity of the emotional relationships represented affects that family members could not tolerate and were therefore projecting onto the therapists. But they could find no way to articulate this hypothesis and reintroduce the projected affects into the therapy in a way that would join them with the therapeutic task. That is, they were unable to negotiate a shared interpretation with the family.

After several months of vain attempts at interpretation in both individual and family therapies and similarly fruitless attempts at limit setting by halfway house staff, Fred's individual therapist had an unusual experience. Ordinarily a very sound sleeper, he awoke at 3:00 A.M. in a fury. In his dream, he had profoundly identified with Fred and had been in a rage at Fred's parents, who had gone off unpredictably, leaving him alone. The therapist's analysis of this dream over the next several weeks was facilitated by his own regression, which took him through aspects of his past and his relationship with his parents. He began to realize that his detachment and despair represented a familiar defensive avoidance of his own anger, protest, and grief at being abandoned. He increasingly recognized that he was angry at Fred for abandoning him in the therapy. The dream provided him with deeper insight into the Browns' responses in their parental role, since part of his own anger at and withdrawal from Fred arose from his annoyance at not being responded to in his role as therapist. With this perspective, he began to reexamine his role in the family therapy. He suspected that Fred might be experiencing feelings of abandonment that he was finding impossible to bear. Fred therefore might be responding defensively to the therapist's and his parents' abandonment by identifying with them, manifestly by abandoning the therapist. Implicitly, Fred might be wanting to know if the therapist could manage such unbearable affects. The therapist's identification with Fred in the family meeting intensified his response, since he also felt abandoned by the parents. He began to feel like a poorly prepared babysitter left to manage a child who was taking out on him his anger at the parents.

When the Browns announced another trip in a family session later that month, the therapist reviewed both their absences and Fred's and noted somewhat sharply that family members were continually leaving and abandoning each other and him and that *he* did not like it. Mrs. Brown tentatively asked the therapist if he were angry at them. Before the therapist could respond, Fred, who had appeared to be lost in dissociated thought, broke in with a sudden outburst of anger at the parents and spoke at length in a new and quite connected manner about his long-standing confusion about whether his parents were or were not available. He recalled numerous instances from his childhood of sudden, unplanned parental trips and bewildering placements with babysitters or relatives. He talked of his sense that he had done something wrong each time they left, of his certainty that they would never return, and of his fantasies of running away to find them.

The parents, astonished by this outburst, said they had never known that he objected to their trips. They revealed their fears of upsetting the children by discussing their trips ahead of time and their insistence on talking only to the babysitters when they telephoned home "for fear of upsetting the children." Fred commented that he had never known they had called. Mother spoke of her sense that she and her husband could just disappear for trips and the children would not mind very much. Father, with great sadness, talked of his perception that his children did not like him very much and of his conviction that all he had to offer them was physical comfort and financial support, that his presence was not significant. In the couple's therapy, the parents began to recognize that their defensive withdrawal from Fred represented both the consequence of an unconscious projection of their own vulnerabilities onto him and an avoidance (like the therapist's) of their anger and pain that their son was not responding to their loving overtures.

In individual therapy, Fred reviewed these childhood events in greater detail. The therapist, who had by now become familiar with these sudden abandonments by both adolescent and parents, was able to communicate his understanding of the patient's bewilderment, confusion, and rage as well as to interpret the repetition of these early experiences in the therapeutic relationship between Fred and himself.

In the following family meeting, the adolescent turned to his parents with tears of rage and sadness and told them that he did not know them at all, that they were strangers to him, and that he had no sense of who he himself was. He revealed his confusion, despair, and loneliness and began to talk of his long-standing feeling that he had to take care of himself and could depend on no one. In response, both parents recalled similar feelings of isolation in their own childhoods and were able to see the lack of contact in their current family.

Throughout Fred's childhood his parents had failed to respond to his dependent needs empathically. Thus, Fred and his parents were unconsciously colluding in an unempathic dependent relationship that could not be acknowledged. As a result the family manifested the rage that often accompanies affronted dependency: Fred's suicide attempts and the parents' assertion of the insignificance of their parental role. Because

Fred's self-destructive violence was not a clear extension of his dependency needs, these needs were difficult to perceive.

The therapist assigned to Fred for individual work was especially caught up in this interchange. Yet because of its powerful collusiveness, he observed only violence, aggression, loss, and sadness as discrete feelings. He did not grasp that the system as a whole (not just individual relationships) was generating these feelings or that these feelings provided evidence of how poorly the family's task was being managed. In particular he did not realize that although the parents had not responded to Fred's dependent needs, the three of them had developed a highly collusive unconsciously dependent system. Focusing on the more manifest anger, he did not notice the deeper connections between family members. However, his regression in the interest of uncovering his connections to family members' experience, the violence of his dream, and his reflection on it exposed enough of his own feelings and their congruence with the family dynamics for him to begin working again with the parents and the boy. Then they could begin together to construct a rudimentary holding environment using empathic response (the shift occurred through a conjunction of individual work with Fred and Fred's work with his parents in the family meeting). What had previously been boundary-breaking actions (Fred's violence, the missed appointments) were transformed into subjective experiences that could be offered, shared, appreciated, and interpreted.

The second facet of the holding environment—containment—was also directly related to the therapist's intervention within the family system. In the Brown family, feelings of guilt, rage, despair, and loneliness were missing from the interactions between family members. Parental guilt, isolation, and feelings of inadequacy were denied, acted out, and projected. The therapist's task in this situation included the need to contain these emotions and help put them into perspective without becoming overwhelmed by them. The therapist had to believe that despite the parents' feelings of inadequacy, they truly desired an improved relationship with their son. Similarly, the therapist needed to recognize that Fred's violence was a desperate communication of his suffering, trust that the parents could survive a confrontation, and know that continued contact was essential.

The cases we have just reviewed involve families in trouble. But the issues they raise illuminate our basic premise: If the need for emotional connectedness is not satisfied, collective human endeavor is impossible.

And the source of the resulting difficulties cannot be found in individuals alone. Instead, we must look to the dynamically interactive structures that individuals create in order to make sense of their behavior. The power of these dynamics within the family is illuminated by the therapist's occasional unwitting and unconscious involvement in the system.

The human longing for and unconscious creation of connectedness mean that our lives as individuals cannot be considered apart from the contexts in which they are lived by necessity (for example, with parents or with children) or by choice (for example, through marriage or joining an organization). It finds its major expression, therefore, in families and at work. But families and other organizations are two of the places where distress is most frequently articulated. To move beyond mere expressions of dismay, we need to discover ways to link the basic human need for connectedness with the dynamic structures that are required for collaborative work.

The concept of the holding environment and its focus on the task of the organization appears to be one such structure. But before we can further develop this notion, certain questions must be raised. To what extent can these ideas, which derive from therapy, be applied to other contexts in social and organizational life? Can we legitimately broaden our interpretive model, derived from psychoanalysis and the study of the family, to encompass an environment so practical and rationally constructed as the workplace? Do individuals carry aspects of their experience within the family with them into other organizations? How can an outsider have an impact on organizational dynamics that are broader than those of the individual? To pursue these questions, we must look more closely at organizations.

Part II

Moving to

Organizations

The three chapters in this section provide a transition from the family to larger organizations. In chapter 5 we present a way of linking our clinical investigation of the family to its parallels in organizational life. In chapter 6, we describe the interpretive stance in detail. We contend that deep and often hidden connections exist between the individual and the group and that individual experience, if scrutinized in relation to role, can reveal central aspects of the larger organization. Our description of this stance is offered as a way to contend with the general experience of being lost in familiar places. It takes individual experience in role as the primary source of data about the dynamic functioning of the organization. The task of the organization then becomes the framework within which to uncover the relatedness of people in their various roles to the organization as a whole. In chapter 7 we present an extended illustration of the application of the interpretive stance to an organization.

5 ○ From the Family

to Larger Organizations

The case studies of two families have suggested how we perceive and begin to interpret the contemporary experience of being lost in the familiar. Our lives, however, are not lived solely within the family. As we mature, other structures and contexts impinge upon us. In this chapter we offer ways of connecting the phenomenology of family life to that of larger organizations. In subsequent chapters we will explore through extended case studies ways of using the interpretive stance in these organizational settings.

As we become aware of our psychological complexity as individuals and begin to assume that we may have access to at least some of this complexity, we may also begin to believe that it is possible to understand why people behave as they do. On the other hand, the more we become aware that our experience of ourselves is affected by others, not just in our families but also in the larger contexts in which we live, the less sure we seem to become about where our individual experience begins and ends.

The experience of a group of social workers illustrates this dilemma. At one point in their training they attempted to expand their view of their clients beyond the family setting to include the clients' connections to larger systems. The premise was that their clients' personal problems might partially reflect and symbolically represent an aspect of their working contexts. The social workers were also asked to consider how they themselves were not just individuals but representatives of a larger organizational setting (in this case, the state). With these clarifications, they could see how each interaction between client and social worker was also an interaction between groups. They were initially enthusiastic about this framework, which shed new light on problems in their profession. But soon some began to lose confidence in this approach. The cause of their despair was eventually uncovered. Surviving as a confused social worker had been difficult enough; now, however, they had entered a larger world. They began to feel that before they could do anything with an individual client they had to engage in what they described as "world therapy." This new perspective caused the boundaries of their role as social worker to seem distressingly fragile. They developed a sense of uncertainty about themselves and the work for which they were being trained. They felt caught in an unresolvable dilemma: either they adopted the proposed stance and felt overwhelmed, or they ignored it and continued to work in a way that they now knew to be less than fully effective. No third option was apparent (Barnes 1984). These social workers were feeling lost in the familiar, for when their analytically derived stance of interpreting the individual was located in a wider and apparently unlimited context, feelings of naivete and impotence resulted.

The danger is that we, like the social workers, will lose track of what we think we know in our search for links with something larger. Our aim in this chapter, therefore, is to describe how individual experience initially formed within the family setting can be related to a larger organizational context without losing the integrity of the individual. To achieve this we need to develop a conceptual structure that will provide the two fundamental elements that we have already discerned as essential for the emergence of the individual—sufficient containment so that boundaries can be clarified and an experience in a role articulated such that empathic interpretation is possible.[1]

Any interpretation must draw together three interrelated complexities —the individual, the context, and the connections between them. As our study of the family has shown, any interpretive model for human behavior must allow us to interpret individual and group interactions congruently. Isolating the individual from the context of the group, as some analytically based interpretations tend to do, may encourage valuable self-knowledge, but it may also cause us to lose touch with a major aspect of reality—that we each experience continuing and changing interactions with other people within a multitude of contexts. Similarly, a model must enable us to evaluate group phenomena—the way any set of people behaves—and provide connections to the demands and structures of an organization (Handy 1988).

THE INDIVIDUAL, THE FAMILY, AND THE ORGANIZATION

We seek to develop an interpretive stance that connects individuals and their experiences with a major context for those experiences —organizations. We have already illustrated how the experiences of various individuals within the family provide the data that allows the family to rediscover itself and its task. But the individual, the family, and the organization have much in common. The usefulness of drawing attention to these connections is most clearly articulated by Miller and Rice (1967):

> The theories of human behavior and of activity systems are in many respects analogous. Like a system of activities, an individual or a group may be seen as an open system, which exists and can exist only through processes of exchange with the environment. Individuals and groups, however, have the capacity to mobilize themselves at different times into many different kinds of activity systems; and only some activities are relevant to the performance of the tasks of the various enterprises. . . . [We see] the individual, the small group and the larger group . . . as progressively more complex manifestations of a basic structural principle. Each can be described in terms of an internal world, an external environment, and a boundary function which controls transactions between what is inside and what is outside (pp. 14–15).

We find this approach cogent and valuable. However, since most organizational theory originated within the world of business, the development of a theory exploring the connections between organizations, families, and individuals has been limited. The activities of business organizations have been viewed largely in terms of economics and politics. This focus on abstract notions so far removed from individual and family experience may even have contributed to the sense of being lost that we are interested in examining. For most people, experience in a business organization constitutes a major dimension of their lives. For them the exploration of values and beliefs in that setting is crucial and far from abstract. Profound emotions, both conscious and (as we shall also argue) unconscious, are involved.

Psychoanalytic perspectives in the organizational area have focused primarily on two issues: the motivation of workers and the connection between personal psychology and group activity. The psychoanalytic model contains certain primary notions—in particular, transference (the recreation in present relationships of projections from childhood relationships), countertransference (the feelings experienced by those who receive these projections), and projective identification (the encouragement of feelings in others that correspond to disavowed aspects of one's own internal conflicts)—all of which may be discerned in family, group, and organizational processes. We have already seen the impact of these phenomena on family pathology and task performance. But it may be that in organizations these notions may involve aspects of the organization's necessary and legitimate activity that are liable to be overlooked or inadvertently discounted. We will explore this proposition in detail in our extended case study in chapters 8, 9, and 10.

When the human components of organizations are considered, two distinctive and centrally important characteristics emerge: imagination and self-reflection. Imagination plays an important role in our development both as individuals and in groups, and it is central to the therapeutic interventions discussed earlier in this book. Given the appropriate conditions, for instance, Fred Brown (see chapter 4) can make an imaginative leap from his rigid and inarticulate anger to his relationships with his parents. By creatively linking his own emotional experience to that of family members and helping the family to redraw a series of boundaries, the therapist helped the family members to free their imaginations from their unconscious strictures. Unless such nonlogical but effective connections are made, some problems will not and probably cannot be solved.

When we exercise our imagination, we interact more critically with our environment. Life is genuinely interactive, consisting of two-way traffic between us and our varied contexts. Imagination is not the same as curiosity, but it has the same effect of preventing ultimate certainty. Indeed, we have noted that pathological certainty in family interaction destroys the ability to see (and therefore to imagine) anything new about oneself, other people, or the context. When, however, the capacity either to be curious or to exercise imagination is rediscovered, the process of negotiated interpretation can begin.

A second key human capacity is that of self-reflection. The subject, "I", is capable of reflecting upon itself as the object, "me." This ability to stand outside ourselves is the basis upon which reflection is possible, thought can occur, and change can be achieved.

Imagination and self-reflection are two primary conditions for our psychological development. We become aware of ourselves as objects, but our imaginative capacities allow us to move beyond a fixed sense of ourselves. We do not have to be what we find ourselves being. Nor need we experience the world outside ourselves as confining; rather, we can see it as providing opportunities for virtually limitless response. We speak of ideas "striking us" or "coming to us." Our better moments involve our interaction with our contexts, whether through reflecting on our behavior or imaginatively placing ourselves in our environment. Because we can make imaginative leaps and perform creatively, we can and do change both ourselves and our environment. We have seen how a family can imaginatively recreate itself in the process of change. The issue may be raised whether an organization, too—like a human organism—can imaginatively reflect upon itself.

To speak of an institution's self-understanding or imaginative action is misleading if not bizarre. It is not impossible, however, to speak of an organization's being interpreted by individuals using their experiences in their roles to reflect collaboratively and imaginatively upon the whole. This, for example, is what happens when a consultant is invited to work with an organization. He views the organization as a unit and uses that view as a reference point against which the participant members can test their experiences. In so doing we may say that he helps the organization to engage in self-reflection. Then, through the energy of its human components, the organization may engage in corporate change, which is greater than the sum of individual changes on the part of the members or participants.

INDIVIDUAL EXPERIENCE, THE GROUP, AND THE ORGANIZATION

To explore the possibility that organizations, as collections of imaginative individuals, can reflect upon themselves, we must articulate the crucial linking points between the experience of the individual, the group, and the organization. For the beginnings of these connections, we turn to a theory proposed by W. R. Bion, whose seminal thinking on groups brought the individual and the group together in a distinctive fashion.

Bion studied groups of strangers given the task of studying themselves. Unlike the family, with its clearly articulated task, Bion's groups were more diffusely organized. This led him to uncover more generalized themes about group life that apply both to the family and to organizations. Bion (1961) hypothesized that a human group, like an individual, functions at two complementary levels, which he called "work" and "basic assumption." The corresponding levels for the individual are conscious rational activity ("work") and irrational and unconscious motivations ("basic assumption"). Much of the time, these levels are in uneasy tension; occasionally, they come into conflict, with potentially disastrous results. For instance, a dependent attachment to leaders can be usefully mobilized in the service of competent followership. If, on the other hand, irrational dependency interferes with an adequate assessment of a leader's destructive aims, disaster may result. When these levels are in harmony, then organizationally effective working and personally satisfying living can result.

Bion proposed and described three basic unconscious assumptions that appeared to interfere with task performance. For our purposes we need not discuss these in detail. We offer brief descriptions here, and we will examine their effects in the remainder of the chapter.

1. *Dependence*: the unconscious and shared assumption in groups that members come together to gratify their dependency needs rather than to work. Dependence recalls the unconscious human search for the assurance that our psychological selves are secure enough to allow us to take risks. We have already examined this need in our discussion of the importance of a holding environment. There is, however, always a danger that the dependence necessary for collaboration may become irrational. Then some institution, idea, or individual may be unconsciously elevated to the status of an ultimate resource for gratification and individuals may surrender any sense of their own responsibility. There is nothing very controversial about this dynamic. It is in many ways the most familiar and most powerful. There are few people who on reflection cannot identify dependence—rational and irrational—as having been discernible and problematic in their experience in organizations.

2. *Fight/Flight*: the shared unconscious assumption, often carried out through action, that members are gathered to fight with or flee from leadership rather than to join in effective work. The two elements of this assumption are linked—not either "fight" or "flight" but both"fight and flight." In everyday discourse, we often separate the parts; we speak of people as either fighting or running away from authority or from work. But as Bion correctly observed, the underlying dynamic of both attitudes is the same. Individuals who are caught up in this assumption are volatile and ambitious. Yet this dynamic also contributes to making groups and organizations creative and exhilarating places to work.

For example, we discussed in the Introduction how the faculty of

McLean Hospital mobilized the fight/flight dynamic to preserve the integrity of their institution at a time of crisis. Because of the ambiguity and the sense of risk involved with this dynamic, it is not an easy one to harness for rational work activity. In particular, since fight/flight is always experienced in relation to something seen as "bad," it is powerfully mobilized by projections. Thus, it often becomes crucial for individuals to notice what projections are being mobilized, if this dynamic is to be harnessed to creative achievement. In the McLean story, for instance, projections about insensitivity, greed, and indifference were identified by the medical staff and the trustees and stimulated a productive discussion about the values involved in patient care and profit making.

3. *Pairing*: the shared unconscious assumption that the group is organized to produce an ideal pair that will develop a miraculous solution to problems as opposed to facing and overcoming difficulties through collaborative effort. In "pairing" we discern a deepening of dependence, which, instead of being focused on an individual, group, or idea is focused on a pair of individuals or on two linked groups. The expectation is that the two individuals or the two groups will somehow produce a reliable solution to the organization's problems. For example, many people believe that the political union of blacks and whites in contemporary South Africa will miraculously solve the problems of an endangered society.

By linking rational and irrational processes, Bion's theory permits us to draw a common interpretive model for both the individual and the group. This does not mean an identical model, but one that uses the common data of feelings and offers a common basis of interpretation, without reducing the individual merely to a symptom of the group or the group to an expanded notion of the individual. Their interaction is affirmed.

Beyond the group and the organization, however, looms the even larger and more incoherent "society." Bion examined the context of Great Britain during the first half of this century and suggested that each of the three underlying assumptions was embodied in a particular social institution: dependency in the church, which offered ultimate reassurance; fight/flight in the army; and pairing in the aristocracy, as the public attention focused on their marriages indicated. In part IV, we shall apply Bion's theory to even larger-scale phenomena.

THE INSTITUTION-IN-THE-MIND

The organization is composed of the diverse fantasies and projections of its members. Everyone who is aware of an organization, whether a member of it or not, has a mental image of how it works. Though these diverse ideas are not often consciously negotiated or agreed upon among the participants, they exist. In this sense, all institutions exist in the mind, and it is in interaction with these in-the-mind entities that we live. Of course, all organizations also consist of certain real factors, such as other people, profits, buildings, resources, and products. But the meaning of these factors derives from the context established by the institution-in-the-mind. These mental images are not static; they are the products of dynamic interchanges, chiefly projections and transferences. Transference is not limited to the analytic situation; nor is it solely an interpersonal phenomenon of everyday life. Sarah Bienegro, for instance, found herself reacting to the hospital's restrictions on her friends as if the institution were her family failing to recognize her needs. This was an institutional transference.

Much thinking about organizations has derived from work done with and for commercial and industrial enterprises. Though much of our own conceptual work has involved organizations more obviously concerned with feelings (families, hospitals, churches), we do not wish to base a method of approaching the variety of institutions-in-the-mind solely upon the dynamic structures of the family or upon organizations whose explicit task concerns handling people and their welfare. The fundamental question remains: Can we develop a coherent model by which we can attempt to interpret individual, group and organizational experience, of whatever origin? Bion's theory of basic assumptions provides a beginning. But his theory applies to all groups. The issue of how these dynamics shift in relation to particular organizational tasks as context remains cloudy.

In our earlier study of the family, we found that our hypothesized family task of furthering individual development provided us with a context in which we could deepen our understanding of underlying family irrationality. Are there similar tasks in different work settings that will allow us to refine Bion's notions of unconscious assumptions? Organizations may appear to have more concrete tasks than families. But it may be that in some way their tasks, like the family's task, may also relate to collective human development. A study of the emotional texture of organizational life in different settings may give us sufficient perspective to discern such larger tasks.

We will examine three representative types of organizations (commercial, therapeutic, and voluntary) and describe how collective human interaction may operate there. Just as the structure of the family has become more chaotic, organizational structure is changing, too, and prototypes capture only general themes.

Commercial Organizations

We use the label "commercial" loosely. These organizations produce a profit and so provide the means of livelihood for participants directly and for others indirectly through taxation. Sometimes such organizations deal directly with people and their needs; transportation companies are examples of this. But for these organizations, people are chiefly considered units in the system. Passengers, for instance, are units to be processed; staff are the functionaries who handle the "passenger units." In these systems, roles are carefully assigned and defined.

In commercial organizations, the idea of the institution-in-the-mind plays a central role. Because there is an easily definable series of goals —earning a profit, producing a product, ensuring the happiness of the workers and the enthusiasm of the shareholders, and so on—there is a temptation to decide that one of these constitutes the defining characteristic of the organization. When this happens, the larger social task of the institution can be obscured. Then, the dynamic interconnection between those outside the organization and those within it, which can help to provide a clearer definition of the organization's task, may be overlooked.

Although personal contact, affection, even loyalty, and, above all, communication are discussed and encouraged, workers are often held together solely by a sense of their function in relation to the larger enterprise ("I design airplane engines for Lockheed."). They therefore feel connected to the "institution-in-the-mind" without necessarily discovering what the institution stands for.

One consequence, however, is that people in separate roles may find themselves filled with feelings but with no clear place to which to connect them, except to themselves and to their own group. This may account for the way in which, for example, certain types of groups—managers, or production engineers, or data processors—become insular. They relate their feelings first to themselves and their relationships to each other as a professional group or as a subgroup in the organization rather than to some larger task. In addition, because the organization seems to be composed of a series of well-defined groups, the opportunity for projective behavior is that much greater. Feelings, which provide vital data about the state of the individual and the organization, tend to be managed through projections, rather than being identified, acknowledged, and interpreted with a view toward their significance for the more comprehensive work of the organization.

Therapeutic Organizations

Today a multitude of organizations offer care and welfare. Like the staff of the hospital we discussed in the Introduction, their members are often in conflict over whether their primary product is patient care or profit. Sometimes these organizations have even been run according to the model of a commercial organization, with emphasis placed on their output.

If we apply the notion of a product to therapeutic organizations, then the product is human beings *along with* their feelings. One frequent result is that for the staff of the institution the line between their own feelings and those of the people to whom they are providing care becomes blurred. Sometimes the organization's management protects its staff from this confusion by arranging supervision, support groups, and the like. But parallel with this runs an unconscious structuring of such organizations for defense against developing anxiety (see Menzies 1960 and chapters 8, 9, and 10).

In contrast with staff in commercial organizations, who are chiefly involved with the institution-in-the-mind, those in therapeutic organizations live under constant pressure to deal with personal relationships. Since their task involves care and is consequently loaded with emotional factors, relationships become the primary mode of connecting, not only between staff and patients or clients, but also among staff members and within staff groups. The staff may assume that if each person can be understood or if all relationships can be perfected, then any severe problems of organizational life will decline or disappear. This view underestimates the significance of the organization as a whole.

In institutions providing care, the roles of "patient" and "staff" are constantly in danger of being eroded and collapsed into a general heading of "feeling human." Staff members may consciously contribute to this erosion by assuming that boundary formation and role differentiation interfere with empathic understanding. Alternatively, they may protect themselves from emotional overload by drawing rigid personal boundaries that obscure their role boundaries and lead to unconscious and therefore unmanaged and uninterpreted identifications with patients. This confusion about boundaries may interfere with the staff members' capacity to extrapolate from their individual role experience and to reflect on the life of the organization as a whole, its effectiveness, and the usefulness of its activity. In chapter 9, we look at an example of such an organization as a way to illuminate the broader experience of being lost in a familiar place.

Voluntary Associations

A third type of organization includes churches, social clubs, professional organizations, and small cause groups, such as political pressure groups and associations that fill gaps in the standard or established provision of care—for example, associations for sufferers from specific illnesses or disabilities and their families. Such groups often fund research and provide support for victims.

These organizations are, like the therapeutic ones, often concerned with feelings, but with one major difference. Those who provide the feelings and those who generate the context in which they are handled are one and the same. The space between these two roles, therefore, is easily obliterated. Such organizations tend to be unable to respond well to outside pressures, such as political demands to broaden their framework (for example, efforts to link antiwar organizations of different commitments). They internalize them and react in irrational ways.

In these organizations, individuals are not hired for particular skills, but instead assume roles because of personal interest or interpersonal connections. Voluntary associations are therefore closest in style to families. Although such organizations do not pretend to further the development of any specific individual, they do promote an individual's development in his role as volunteer and are more generally concerned with helping a particular aspect of society to reflect on itself and develop. Thus since the person concerned is often selected for hidden psychological reasons, family dynamics without blood ties prevail.

Organizations, just like individuals, vary greatly. Although they sometimes appear to be monolithic, almost isolated entities, with no links to one another or to the society in which they are set, certain connections do exist.

Bion's insights about the individual and the group provide a way to connect dynamic human functioning with group and organizational processes. In his theory, neither the personality of individuals nor the distinct type of organization is a key factor. What is important is both the dynamic interchange between members in relation to the group's task and its leadership—this provides the focus of attention and the basis on which hypotheses are generated. But in different organizations, these interchanges occur at different task boundaries. So we must expand Bion's theory to include the particular qualities of the institutions and the personalities of the individuals involved. First, however, we must provide an interpretive framework that will lend coherence to our inquiry.

It is to this inquiry that we now turn. We propose to discuss neither individuals, nor groups, nor organizations as such. Instead, we shall explore interaction, the way individuals and institutions act with, among, and for each other. This exploration will clarify how individuals are connected to organizations and how organizations are related to the larger structures of society. In pursuing this inquiry, we shall use the model of individuals within the family, focusing on their capacities for imagination and self-reflection, as a way of thinking about organizations and how we are linked to them. But we must remember that we do not pretend to know (certainty) but rather that we interpret (hypothesize).

6 ○ The Interpretive

Stance

I n our studies of the borderline patient, we saw that family members'
inability to value a child's experience contributed to their shared
sense of being lost in the world of the familiar. An individual's
experience provides the primary data source for any interpretive effort,
yet by itself it is incomplete; in order to be interpreted adequately, the
individual's experience needs to be placed in context. We can see this
clearly in the following account.

A psychiatric clinic appointed a young woman to introduce a new
program in child psychotherapy. She was herself a trainee in psychology,
so she had to cope with the clinic's expectations as well as the general
suspicion that such an inexperienced person could not competently introduce a new program. About the same time a new senior doctor was
appointed. He publicly proclaimed his support for her approach. Her
own perception, however, was that he was ambivalent about it. Her
anxieties began to focus around one small piece of repeated behavior.
The doctor would come into her office, which contained only her desk
and some chairs for the children being treated in the clinic. While talking with her he would sit on the desk and rest his feet on the chairs. The
trainee found this extremely annoying, but, aware of her junior position,
felt she could not discuss it with him. She therefore held the experience
within herself and reported it to her psychoanalyst. The analyst suggested that she might be reexperiencing in this interaction with the doctor her early angry reaction to her father who "stepped on the child" in
her without loving it or respecting its value. Though this interpretation

resonated with part of her experience, it did not connect with other parts, chiefly those aspects that involved her role in the clinic. She felt but could not articulate to herself or her analyst a vague sense that something important was being lost.

On reflection, we can begin to see what was happening: the behavior of another person (the senior doctor) was stirring aspects of the trainee's self with which she was coming to terms. Her use of this bit of data with her analyst was proper and reasonable in relation to their task of better understanding her life. However, since she and the doctor also had symbolic roles in the clinic, the interaction between them might also have represented an organizational dynamic concerning commitment to or ambivalence about a new treatment. Her irritation with the way the doctor apparently trod on the children (putting his feet on their chairs) might thus have been potentially as useful for the organization as for her private self.

The trainee's difficulty was that the more she attempted to grasp what was happening in terms of her own dynamics (or, for that matter, in terms of her projections about the personality of the doctor), the more problematic the experience became. In her familiar places—her transference world with her analyst and her professional world as a child psychotherapist (and no doubt in other roles, too)—she felt increasingly lost. She was unable to use her reactions to engage with and change her environment. She needed a way to gain perspective both on herself (with her analyst's help) and on herself-in-role within the clinic. It was not a question of one or the other; both facets belonged to her world, and an interpretation that incorporated both was needed. In the absence of connecting interpretations, she was finding herself increasingly confused about the significance of her experience within a primary organization in her life—her place of work.

This is a problem we all have in everyday life: disentangling context and personal experience quickly enough to achieve the integration needed to act effectively, or indeed even to think clearly. We need a stance for interpretation.

By "stance for interpretation," we are not talking about a specialized stance toward organizational interpretation that formally appointed consultants might adopt. We are instead proposing a method that individuals might use to integrate an evaluation of their experience (which the psychoanalyst provided in the story about the trainee) and an interpretation of that experience from the context of their institutional role (a form of group consultation). Integrating experience and context could lead to a thoughtful study of the organization, a deeper commitment to it and, in collaboration with the linked interpretations of others, to organizational change.

The notion of "role" is a key element in the integrative interpretative stance that we are advocating, as the story of the trainee demonstrates. The trainee found that her assigned role provided the crucial link between her self (in analysis) and her context (in the clinic). A role is not a position that is assumed, much less one that is "played." Instead, a role provides the framework in which person and context meet. In our model, role is a function of the organization's task. Thus, for example, the role of "father" derives from the developmental task. The role of psychotherapist may be a function of the therapeutic task that is institutionalized in a clinic. However, similar roles may be occupied by different people who experience them in differentiated ways. Thus, although interpretation of personal experience affirms the uniqueness of the individual, placing that experience in the context of a role affirms the connection to the organization. Such affirmation is an aspect of an organizational holding environment.

When we discussed the development of roles within the family, we noted the significance of a holding environment that allows for containment of impulses and affirmation of individual experience as it interacts with the experiences of others. The essence of this, it will be recalled, is that the holding environment is negotiated. Although it may appear that the mother provides a holding environment for the child, in fact there is mutuality in the arrangement. The loved child also has an affirming role within the parent-child unit, which is the initial organization that manages the developmental task. The holding is created collaboratively.

The same applies in other settings. Membership in an organization may create a shared notion of task that sustains individuals in their roles. So long as we have a sense of what we belong to, we can struggle to discover the task the organization is performing and the roles we have in relation to that task. By creating, managing, and developing a shared task, one function of organizations and institutions is to provide a holding environment similar to that first experienced in the family. But just as such holding is negotiated in the family, so, too, is that provided by organizations. Members can create these holding qualities through the negotiation of a shared culture in which the individual's experience as articulated through his organizational role is assumed to illuminate underlying values, characteristics, or assumptions of the organization. Once this culture has been created, individuals can begin to link their experi-

ences through interpretations, creating a shared picture of the organization that both affirms individual experience and provides a starting point
for organizational development and change.

One outcome of this organizational holding is the intense group loyalty that can emerge in role-determined groups. So, for instance, players
on a football team, with their different abilities and personal experiences, become deeply connected to each other and to the larger team in
relation to the shared task of winning. By attempting to interpret individual experiences that are acquired and generated in role, therefore,
individuals may discover a similar depth of connection between themselves and their institutional settings and may find themselves once again
in familiar places. This is the case with life in the family. It is also, we
suggest, a consequence of adopting such an interpretive stance in relation to all of our contexts and the roles we occupy in them.

INTERPRETING EXPERIENCE IN ROLE

For interpreting how our individual experience takes on additional meaning in the context of institutions, we propose a broad, self-
reflective model. We call this model "the interpretive stance." The interpretive stance has two features of primary importance.

First, the stance is speculative, imaginative, and heuristic. In other
words, it allows the possibility of proceeding from one hypothesis to
another hypothesis rather than from uncertainty to certainty. But these
characteristics are not unfortunate problems to be solved or irrationalities to be avoided; rather, we begin to recognize them as realities that
link individuals with their social settings. Indeed, these qualities reflect
the ambiguities and uncertainties of life as we know it.

At any given moment in any social or organizational setting, one or
two of our roles are likely to be prominent in our minds. Most of us
conceptualize our roles in some way and connect these concepts to our
sense of our organizations. These concepts thus become the temporary
structures in the mind within which and in relation to which interpretations of individual experience may be made. Such interpretation does
not require special expertise or training. Because experience is always
available and is never devoid of context, the interpretive stance is always
possible. Though profound emotional or organizational disturbances
can shift us from this ideal, these shifts should be temporary. Given the
opportunity for reflection, even disturbing experiences provide vital data
for the initial interpretation that can facilitate our discovery of connec-

tions to others. Using these connections, we can enhance our usefulness to our various organizational contexts, whether domestic, professional, or in society at large.

The second feature of our stance is that it allows us to connect hypotheses that originate in different sectors of our lives without producing confusion. The experience of fragmentation is a significant part of feeling lost. Here, the "familiar place" is "I"—we are truly lost when we feel fragmented within ourselves. Since individual experience is, by definition, indivisible within the individual, the use of different roles as contexts for interpretation allows different aspects of the individual's experience to be creatively connected.

An example may clarify these points. A company's stated policy is that it is an equal opportunity employer. Women and men, as far as anyone can tell, seem to be treated equally on the basis of proven competence. However, as a result of difficulties with her husband, a female staff member may be acutely aware of her gender experience—women are devalued or powerless; women are always put upon; women are treated nicely but not seriously. Because each of these expressions generalizes in terms of "all women," this gender formulation may obscure the thrust of her own feelings—"I am devalued" and so on. We may locate her experiences in the context of the overlapping roles that she occupies —wife, mother, spouse, lover, but also business woman, executive, member of the company. Rather than trying (probably in vain) to disentangle these roles and claim that the experience of gender-related difficulty is related particularly to one facet of her life—probably problems at home —the interpretive stance would suggest the potential usefulness of reflecting on these experiences in the context of her role within the company.

Examining her experience, from wherever it arises, through the filter of her organizational role could offer clues about particular aspects of her work setting. So, for example, she may discover that in her organization women are mostly employed in underpaid support systems, such as secretarial and housekeeping departments. Or she may note aspects of vacation scheduling that reveal an underlying, and hitherto unsuspected, organizational bias. The possibilities are endless. If others within the organization participated in a similar reflection, her gender-related issues might not be so easily dismissed by others as her private agenda or simply projected by her as a product of "the system." This interpretive stance assumes that individuals bring their own particular lenses for seeing the nature of the world around them. If a person is feeling acutely the dilemmas of gender issues, she may similarly be bringing, and seeing more acutely, gender-related issues throughout her interpersonal world. The clarity of her perspective, in conjunction with others' related views, might illuminate an aspect of her organization that had not been fully understood.

This broadening of her experience does not diminish the realities of her home situation or her life in other roles. Instead, our interpretive stance takes seriously the indivisibility of individual experience: we cannot really separate our lives into a home part and a work part.

INTERNALIZED CONSULTANCY

We may now begin to examine how individuals may come to be their own consultants—that is, to acquire an internalized interpretive stance. From the perspective provided by one role, individuals can reflect on their experiences and the reason for those experiences in another role. But most, if not all, of us can manage only moments of such reflection, for reflecting consistently on one's experiences would be a daunting prospect, although perhaps an exhilarating one. Although there is always value in self-scrutiny, isolated reflection by individuals would only confirm a sense of being lost in the familiar. This was the case with the young trainee in the clinic.

If, however, the interpretive stance were adopted in that clinic by both the trainee and the senior doctor and interpretations of their interactions were linked, then a central dynamic of the clinic itself (ambivalence toward clinical interventions with young children) might be uncovered. A commitment to developing such a shared interpretation would require all the participants to be willing to consider each person's experience as potentially valid—that is, "How is he or she right?" In this case, taking seriously the senior doctor's belief that placing his feet on the chairs was insignificant may lead him to acknowledge his refusal to join an interpretive culture. Or, if he could articulate further his disconnection from the trainee he might uncover an interpretive connection to his role relationship with the children. Then the trainee's experience, if taken as potentially valid, might lead the pair interpretively into the organization and its task. The doctor might then allow himself to consider the possibility that he was unwittingly enacting in his role a larger organizational ambivalence about treating children. As a result, all involved might develop a deeper grasp of their roles within the clinic. Additionally, we would have the beginnings of an organizational effort to become, in a sense, consultant to itself.

THE MEANING OF "CONSULTANT"

The term *consultant* is widely used today to cover a range of meanings. In some instances, it simply describes an imprecise affiliation, such as when retired politicians—as a form of sinecure—become consultants to industrial companies. Some consultants have or are believed to have greater skills or more specialized knowledge than their associates. For instance, there are consultant engineers or consultant architects. In Great Britain and the United States a consultant is also a senior doctor who holds a tenured post or valued role within a hospital or health service. The criterion common to these examples is status deriving from knowledge, whether actual or presumed.

Our use of the term brings together aspects of these descriptions, but with crucial differences. For example, the areas of expertise are the individuals' sense of themselves and their immediate experiences. And the activities that concern the individual consultants are these inner worlds of experience at the boundaries with the roles they occupy. In other words, individuals who adopt the interpretive stance possess and employ knowledge about themselves and their feelings to examine what is happening to them in a role. The stance is not one of specific cognitive expertise, acquired through study or through years of participation in a particular field. The people who operate with this stance are best described as participant-observers in relation both to their own affective experience and to that reflected from people with whom they have dealings in various organizational roles.

We may, therefore, define consultants as individuals who, in using and interpreting their feelings in their roles, stand both inside and outside themselves, and both inside and outside their organizations. Such consultants become immersed in the dynamics of the organization and consciously try to discover within themselves and through their own experiences a sense of the issues that are important to the organization. They consider how their feelings generated in their roles reflect both organizational process *and* an outside perspective. This provides data from which an interpretation may be attempted (Carr 1985a, pp. 14–18; Miller and Gwynne 1972, pp. 4–15).

Individual experience, which has inevitable priority in all of us, thus progressively becomes a tool for engagement with others around a task.

Three facets of this model link individuals' experiences to what is happening in the organizations in which they participate and to the tasks from which they derive their roles. These three components are: using internal experience, testing interpretations against available data (for example, the interpretations of others) or reality, and discerning the relevant context for interpretation. We shall examine each of these in turn.

Using Internal Experience

Internal experience provides the primary data for the interpretive stance. But such experience is not simply engendered from within. As we have illustrated in the earlier chapters on the family, relationships constitute the crucible within which internal experience is forged. The notion of isolated experience is inconceivable, since we all live in an interpersonal swirl of projections from others that affect our internal lives.

The practical skill the interpretive stance requires is differentiating those feelings that arise from without from those that derive from within. This is a complex task. We are caught up in and contribute to a profoundly interdependent world. As a result, final and assured differentiation is impossible: "I" cannot be defined apart from its interaction with "not I." Since we exist in dynamic interchange with ourselves and one another, to claim personal certainty is to deny an essential uncertainty about life. A fundamental aspect of the interpretive stance for each individual in any setting involves making this internal frame of reference, including its doubtfulness and uncertainty, usable.

Working in organizations engenders feelings in us. It might be useful, then, to consider to what extent organizations have an internal life of their own that can be recognized, so that people can locate themselves and their internal experience in relation to it. Obviously no organization is wholly analogous to an individual. But it is worth testing to see if the attempted comparison produces useful and enlarging ideas.

Organizations may be thought of as collections of persons with experiences. These individuals may use these experiences empathically in the direct service of work, as is the case in organizations such as hospitals, churches, and welfare agencies. But people's experiences may also be indirectly related to work. For example, the introduction of modern technology has frequently generated in people powerful fantasies and feelings about their and others' dehumanization. Such feelings are often displaced and projected, leading to alienation between sectors of an organization. These collective defenses constitute significant aspects of the "internal life" of the organization. Problems with these phenomena are often presented as issues involving communication. However, this is usually only a minor factor in a central dilemma. Communications and relationships are important, but in the contemporary world, even more important is the issue of *relatedness*.

"Relatedness" describes that quality of connectedness that we have with notions that are *only* in the mind, in contrast with "relationship," which indicates at least some actual personal contact. Through our relatedness to aspects of organizations, whether from a limited perspective within them or from the outside, our feelings and behavior may be profoundly affected. For example, in a large industrial firm with many subsidiary companies, the Board of Directors may never meet or see the management and work force of a subsidiary. There is no personal relationship between them, no data that can be examined for reality testing, since there is no actual encounter. Yet it would be foolish to pretend that no connection exists. "Those at the top," though never in direct contact, undoubtedly have an effect on the behavior and performance of the managers and workers of the subsidiary. But this relatedness is not unidirectional: the existence of the subsidiary company also affects the behavior of the directors.

When we discussed projective identification within the family, we noted how projections that occurred in relationships between members not only involved the individuals concerned but also effectively constructed the network that was "the family." This unit could be considered a product of projective behavior that was something more than the sum of the projections. That "something more" was the shared notion in the minds of the family members of "the structured family," which had a task and with which the members in their various configurations were related. Family members' behavior was affected by their connection to their idea of the family at least as much as by specific personal relationships. The therapist was unable to be effective by taking into account solely what he could grasp about relationships within the family and between family members and himself. He also had to consider the less tangible, but no less powerful, impact of the family members' connection with the family unit and with the idea of the task of therapy, from which he derived his role—that is, their senses of relatedness.

In a less emotionally intense context, such as a company and its subsidiary, relationships may not be so discernible. The president and the floorsweeper can scarcely be described as "in a relationship." But they each have ideas about the enterprise in which they participate and so each is 'related to' it and through that to each other. As persons, they are not particularly important to each other; but the roles that each occupies significantly affect each other's behavior, albeit unwittingly. Thus even where no discernible relationship exists, significant shared relatedness exists. And since the company, like the family, does not exist in isolation, we may further discern relatedness between people and many other enterprises with which they have no direct connection. In fact, we would suggest that relatedness is to be found anywhere projections are at work, even if, as frequently in our somewhat impersonal world, no relationship is to be discovered.

Relationship and relatedness, therefore, are key concepts for thinking about interlocking and unexamined projections and internalizations; they have profound impact on our internal experience. They are also ways of conceptualizing central connections between individuals and their roles and society at large. We become so preoccupied with the problems of what we belong to that we overlook the impact that more distant organizations and institutions have on our behavior and hence on our quality of life. The more we become preoccupied with things with which we are in direct contact (that is, "in a relationship"), the easier it is to lose sight of this less immediate, but no less important, dimension of our lives.

When we speak of organizations as entities that handle people's feelings, the context inevitably includes feelings of which they are not consciously aware. However confident an organization may appear in its public presentation, uncertainty and ignorance always exist within it. Questions arise in most organizations, for example, about meaning, identity, survival, and values. Individuals and subgroups who work within the organization and therefore find themselves identified with its various complex dynamics become filled with this uncertainty. Thus, the displaced feelings of individuals and subgroups within the organization provide data concerning not just individuals and their immediate environment but also pressures elsewhere in the organization.

From this perspective, then, we can speak of an organization's "internal life." This is not to say that we conceive of organizations as quasi individuals. We are merely acknowledging that people's feelings and experiences are confined neither to their private lives nor to their roles in organizations. These experiences also reflect the confused dynamics of relatedness that affect the organization, its subgroups, and its wider context. The existence of such a dynamic internal life for both organization and individual makes the first facet of our model of the interpretive stance—using internal experience—both necessary and possible.

Testing Interpretations against Available Data or Reality and Discerning the Relevant Context

The second and third facets of the interpretive model must be discussed together. These facets involve testing reality and discerning the relevant context. The range of experience and fantasies with which each person lives has at least as much of an impact on organizational behavior as any so-called external reality. To test reality within an organizational context, therefore, means to examine the validity assigned to any experience: is it congruent with other people's feelings or is it idiosyncratic? If there is congruence, around what is it coalescing? If there is idiosyncrasy, why this particular type, and why might it be located in this particular individual or role? For us, reality testing is concerned with the creation of shared hypotheses.

Any shared interpretation may be the result of a series of unconscious collusions between those involved and thus may run the risk of being delusional. Therefore, whenever we consider shared interpretations and the need to test them against reality, we also require an external reference or context that transcends individuals and their potential for irrational collusion.

But how do we avoid merely projecting onto this external frame of reference those aspects of ourselves, our organizations, or our roles that we wish to disavow? Although this bind seems serious, in practice it is only apparent. The frame of reference that meets all the requirements we have noted so far, is already available: it is found in the organization's task, that is, the activity the organization exists to perform and around which its members cohere (Miller and Rice 1967).

We have already noted that the notion of organizational task is intimately linked to unconscious connections between people and the way these connections inform behavior. We saw this in our study of the family, whose task we suggested was to facilitate the development of its members. This would not, of course, be how any family would necessarily articulate it. The term *task* here defines the reason for the organization's existence. It is, therefore, a concept, but one that is immediately connected with personal feeling and organizational shape. For instance, in some of our clinical case material we saw that the breakdown of an individual was a symptom of a breakdown in the family organization. This collapse was not simply the result of the sum of individual pathologies. It was a consequence (or a symptom, and therefore an indicator) of the family as a unit or organization losing sight of the reason why it existed in the first place—namely, its task.

Every organization has a task or series of tasks around which people associate. These are not the same as the aims it endorses. These may be of an infinite variety—making money, being affirmed by success, filling the employment roles. But people negotiate individually and collaboratively in relation to something that both transcends these aims and enables them to be pursued—something more than personal relationships —namely, that task, the performance of which assures the organization's continued existence.

The following illustration will clarify the difference between task and aims and show how profound organizational change can occur when aims become confused with task. This may lead to a major transformation or to the organization's demise.

When transatlantic travel was possible only by sea, shipping lines were established to transport passengers and goods across the ocean. At first this was a simple task. It was a major achievement to deliver passengers and cargo safely. Once safety was assured, speed became the key aspect of the task. But since transport by ships remained the only option, transportation remained the task.

During the era of the great liners, competition developed around comfort and luxury. These highly desirable aims gradually, but spuriously, became identified with the survival of the companies, supplanting the task of safe, speedy transportation. They thus failed to perceive the emerging competition that air travel was beginning to offer. Travel by air was largely dismissed by managers of shipping lines because planes could not compare with ships for luxury and comfort. But air travel was in fact committed to the primary task of getting people safely and swiftly across the sea. The shipping companies that lost sight of their task and failed to acquire airlines are no longer in business.

This familiar story demonstrates that, although aims are not unimportant, a perception of task is crucial in maintaining a grip on reality. When the question of task arises, attention is immediately and necessarily directed to the connections (or absence of them) between an organization and its outside world. The idea of task, therefore, inevitably transcends aims and personalities. In this sense individuals do not have tasks, for task is a collaborative notion. Task, therefore, provides a referent that transcends the individual without diminishing his or her significance. It also transcends the organization and affirms it by drawing attention

to its existence in a context. It constitutes not a fixed, unchanging referent but a necessary dynamic point of interpretation.

For example, if we take the family's task to be that of furthering the
development of its members, we see immediately that the significance of
the individual is at the heart of this task—his or her development. Equally,
we may observe how the notion of "furthering individual development"
transcends all the familiar aims families would identify—love, success,
achievements of various kinds. These are not disregarded, but the interface between the family and its context—in this case perhaps not so
much society as an external world of developed individuals—becomes a
point of reference that is neither within the family unit nor beyond it,
but a point around which its present activity can be evaluated.

Organizations and their members frequently and inevitably lose sight
of the notion of task. But without sensitivity to its existence—even when
all are unsure about its precise definition—interpretation is not possible. Reality testing, therefore, does not involve finding a fixed objectiv-
ity. The reality we seek emerges from the process of creating shared
hypotheses about what is going on. Interpretation, therefore, is not offered
but created and thus has a major function both for interpreter and interpreted. This consultation with oneself in role is the core of the stance we
are proposing. The interpretive stance involves identifying individual
experience in the context of a role and using such experience with that
of others to create negotiated interpretations about the organization.

The interpretive stance we are proposing affirms the range of people's
experience and feelings, which may be chaotic and are often projected.
But as in our study of the family, they do not so much need interpretation from outside as a context within which they can be contained,
affirmed, and utilized—a holding environment. This context—in both
families and organizations—is provided by two fundamental notions,
task and role.

Individuals using this stance reflect on their experience as they take
responsibility for their roles. In so doing, both they—as individuals
—and the organization—through its task—are affirmed. The organization develops as its basic mode of scrutiny a style of managed, coordi-
nated self-reflection. The interpretive stance, then, involves grasping a
shared system of meaning by coordinating the two primary frames of
reference we possess: ourselves as individuals, with our experiences, and
our institutions with their tasks and roles.

7 ○ An Organizational

Illustration

This chapter presents an extended illustration that draws together the arguments of the previous two chapters. The example reveals how the interpretive stance itself and the struggle to understand the context provided by the task may transform individuals' confusing experiences into coherent data that are both personally and organizationally relevant.

In the organization to be described, the stated primary task was "to promote the study and development of the technique of group psychotherapy." This professional association, which had been in existence for several decades, had created an event called an "Annual Institute." This was a three-day gathering designed to present the association to a wider public, to provide an educational forum, to attract new members, and to respond to the affiliative needs of the membership. A major feature was the presence of an "outside resource person" who gave a series of workshops focusing on relevant research or a technical theme. One of us (ERS) was invited to present several lectures on adolescents and families. To emphasize the personal aspects of this experience, the report will be given in the first person.

In the invitation, I was asked to accept the title of "Institute Leader" and to present a two-day series of lectures on a theme. The specific meaning of the term *Institute Leader* was not clarified, except that my seminars were to be the "leading issue" of the event. My name and topic figured prominently on the promotional brochure. I was flattered by the

offer and pleased by the opportunity to present my work. I did not pursue my curiosity about the title "leader."

In addition to my lectures, faculty from the association were to conduct structured and unstructured (so-called) paratherapeutic groups,
designed to study group process in relation to themes that reflected the
faculty's own interests. The brochure suggested no relationship between
my lectures and the group activities. In other words, the connection
between what I was invited to contribute and the organization's task
was obscure. Furthermore, it became clear that I was not invited to
attend the final day of the Institute, when various members of the faculty were to discuss my presentations on a panel. When I inquired about
extending my stay in order to participate in this discussion, I was told
quite firmly that it was not necessary.

On my arrival, I was met by one of the organizers of the Institute.
I was introduced to some of the officers of the organization (not the
president), but was neither briefed by nor introduced to the faculty
members who were to be the group leaders. My role seemed to be that
of guest lecturer; the meaning of the title "Institute Leader" remained
obscure.

My lectures were well received and the audience (about three hundred
persons) was responsive, participating actively in the discussion that immediately followed my lecture. My role as guest lecturer carried with it
the experience of distance from the membership, with whom my only
connection was a formal one from a stage. Encounters with members
left me feeling somewhat idealized and kept at arm's length. The warm,
open response I experienced during the lectures contrasted sharply with
the tension I witnessed both between the organization's members and its
leaders and in those who were managing the various events. They invari-
ably appeared hassled, overworked, and irritated. It is worth noting in
passing that this last observation represented my fantasy and denoted an
internal comparison I was drawing at the time between myself and
other "leaders."

One aspect of my presentation was to be a demonstration interview
with a family selected by a member of the organization. Shortly before
the session, one member pointed out the president of the organization,
referring to him (somewhat scornfully, I thought) as "crippled." He did,
on close scrutiny, appear to have a mildly deforming arthritis. The family presented for interview consisted of a mother and two teenage daugh-
ters. The parents were separated and, despite attempts to encourage the
father to attend the consultation, he did not appear. The therapist who

presented the family described the father's absence as evidence of his inadequacy.

The interview focused on the theme of ambivalence toward the absent, and possibly emotionally impaired, father, whose wounded pride had kept him from the interview. His separation from his wife and children had resulted in his being idealized, longed for, and covertly devalued. Part of the following discussion concerned issues of boundary formation in families and the complexities of providing an adequate framework for family therapy that would allow the therapeutic task to proceed. One member of the audience questioned whether an interview structure that excluded the father would make the task of family therapy (with its focus, in this case, on parenting the children) impossible.

In discussing the framework for family work, I became more aware of the problems within the framework of the Institute itself. I found myself internally and symbolically regressing in the service of discovering connections between my experience and the organizational context. I discovered that I identified with the missing father to a degree, in that I, too, was a leader in name only. I began to think about my lack of connection to the process groups that would be meeting between my presentations. The family interview had been so moving, the audience so clearly affected, and the issues so directly approached that I anticipated that some reaction and response would carry over into the intervening group sessions. I asked members of the Program Committee why there was no link between the lectures and the groups and suggested that they might be missing a learning opportunity. Their response was that they had not thought of connecting the two. No one was in charge of managing the interface, which appeared to be an unexamined internal structure that impeded learning and, it seemed, interfered with my role as teacher. I began to feel more like the impaired and excluded father in the family interview who could not participate in his children's development. I realized that my own pride had interfered with my confronting the framework issues more directly at the beginning and that I had been participating, like the father, in my own exclusion. I was beginning to feel lost (unclear about my experience) in a familiar place (the role of lecturer).

On the evening of the first day, following some of my lectures, the family interview, and the initial meetings of the process groups, a cocktail party was held to honor the founders of the organization. I was surprised at the atmosphere of chaos and at the apparent disrespect shown by younger members toward the older generation, manifest in their continuing to talk and drink as the speeches were given. Again I found myself thinking about the day's theme of ambivalence toward absent fathers.

The following morning, one of the founding members greeted me and offered me a paper he had written some years previously on the origins of the organization. The paper described the idea behind the Annual Institutes as an attempt to integrate didactic material and group experience. An outside "Institute Leader" was brought in and given authority to work with the group, both as a teacher and as an organizational consultant and reevaluator. The paper described how this institute leader was originally invited to meet with the group leaders prior to the Institute. They would then continue to meet throughout the three days so that the institute leader could facilitate the integration of the talks and the process groups, bringing participants and faculty together around a shared task of learning and consultation.

The contrast between this description and my experience as a "lecturer" at the current Institute was striking. I felt a strong temporal and symbolic link between myself (as the invited but unincluded "leader") and the author of the paper (the retired and now ignored founder). I developed a hypothesis that the emergence of the role of institute leader as I was now experiencing it might represent the confluence of organizational dynamics. I speculated that the role symbolically reflected a dilemma and that this organization had problems of authorization, task and role definition, and boundary management that could be studied from the perspective of the Annual Institute. Specifically, it appeared to me that the Institute had defined a teaching role that was incorrectly titled and inadequately authorized. My role confusion, it seemed to me, required interpretation and this was leading me in the direction of examining the organization.

Using ideas described in the earlier chapters of this book, I began to theorize that the process groups might each be presenting a piece of the total organizational dilemma as reflected in their relatedness to my role. But I had no data to test this hypothesis. As if by chance, as I was reflecting on this possibility, two members of separate groups approached me to discuss their group experiences.

One young woman recounted her experience of telling her group that she would have to leave before their last meeting. The group had spent the entire session in a fury about her limited commitment. I thought of my own limited time commitment and my departure, scheduled one day before the end of the conference (a fact that was known to the membership). I wondered about the possibility that her group was working on that aspect of their relatedness to me, through displacement onto her. I pondered whether the issue of the leaders' limited commitment in this part-time organization might be important to understanding the system's difficulties.

Then a young man reported his group's dissatisfaction with their group leaders. Members talked of a formlessness in the group's work and speculated openly whether I had been involved at all in the group aspect of the Institute. I considered the possibility that this dissatisfaction might reflect members' awareness (in displacement) of the severed links between poorly authorized leaders and the task of the organization.

Following each morning's lecture, I was invited to meet with half of the faculty (while the other half continued their group work). I was given neither task nor agenda for these meetings, and the faculty members present had no agenda either. The time was spent discussing my formal presentation.

At the end of my lecture series, I met with the other half of the faculty, including the president and several members of the older generation. In my lectures, I had discussed Bion's group theories (see chapter 5) and mentioned my experience as an organizational consultant. One of the older members asked me if I had any observations to share about the organization itself. I replied that I had a number of thoughts about it in relationship to my particular role as institute leader, but that since I had not been invited to study the institution, I was lacking coherent data. The president responded that he would be quite interested in my observations and the rest of the group agreed.

As I reviewed my experience with them, the faculty and group leaders joined me in actively exploring the authority dilemmas I had uncovered. Data were immediately forthcoming from the officers, the members, and the older generation in support of the following themes:

1. There had been a gradual loss of focus on the primary task of the organization. The economic and social pressures of sustaining private practices in a state in which practitioners lived at great distances from one another had left members feeling socially as well as professionally alone. There was some discussion about a possible shift in the primary task of the organization from an intellectual task to a social task, an idea that was supported by the presence of process groups at the Annual Institute without clear content and by the procedure of cocktails and conversations over formal speeches. Loss of links between cognitive and affective work within the organization paralleled the separation between my role and that of the groups. Faculty members felt disconnected,

unguided, unclear about and unsupported in their group work, with no clear place to develop collaborative thinking and new ideas.

2. There was a sense of loss of continuity with the past, with marked ambivalence toward the "founding fathers," who felt unneeded and patronized.

3. Deep splits existed within the organization. Leaders felt impaired, unauthorized, and limited in their roles. They spoke of feeling that they, like me, held only a token function, which was contested by others and unsupported by the membership.

4. There were feelings of loss of direction, depression, and despair about the future of the organization that had not previously been voiced or examined.

This discussion was intense and active. Faculty members found that my experience of my role clearly reflected their organizational experience and confirming data were readily presented. Although the Annual Institute had originally been designed to encourage open evaluation, anxiety about what might be uncovered had contributed to the defensive construction of barriers to prevent scrutiny. This was specifically manifest in the separation of the institute leader from the groups and their discussions. The increasing difficulties of sustaining private practices in the face of widespread competition had led to an unwitting shift in the task of the association in the direction of forming ties of relationships and away from searching for integrated learning. Since this shift had occurred surreptitiously and unconsciously and without negotiation, the leadership was impaired in all of its work. This became most clear in the Annual Institute, where I had experienced it.

Shared unconscious expressions of the impairment within the leadership were elaborated for me in symbolic form over the course of the weekend. These metaphorical guideposts included barring the "leader" from the wrap-up summary, offering the image of a "crippled" leader, expressing contempt for the founding fathers, presenting and intensely discussing a family with an absent father, longing for the leader's presence in the groups, failing to provide an opportunity to develop an in-depth relationship to the institute leader, and separating the affects of idealization (of the lecturer) and fury (in the groups). The data strongly suggested that these unfolding events, capped by the gift to me of the paper describing the association's origins, were unconscious group communications presented for interpretation.

This serendipitous consultation led the organization to reevaluate itself and deeply scrutinize its connections to its environment. This case demonstrates how the interpretive stance both uses and requires serious attention to internal fantasies and associations and their testing against a hypothesis involving the organization's task. The interpretive stance makes use of both the internal workings of the consultant's personality as well as his perceptions and responses to interactive pressures and projections from the group concerning his role. From this perspective, the distinction between the person in the role and the role itself can be scrutinized. The use of internal experience, reality testing, and the task as transcendent reference provides the possibility of interpretation.

In this case, the first object of consultation was the lecturer himself. When he began his work as lecturer he was not expecting to provide consultation to the participants in the meeting or the sponsoring body. His "interpretive stance" was in a sense his own way of life, the stance with which he approached a professional invitation. This case also illuminates the sense of being lost in a familiar place: An expert was invited to lecture to colleagues on his own speciality. He could scarcely be in a more familiar environment, yet he was confused. However, because he did not try to escape that confusion by employing professional defenses, he was able to remain in touch with his feelings and through them with the feelings of his audience. His continued efforts to discern and comprehend the overall task of the association and of the particular event and the faculty's interest in his experience allowed for a negotiated interpretation of the organization. In addition, the interpretive stance enabled him to continue to work as a teacher; assist the organization; and also help others to discern their familiar place, cope with their sense of being lost in it, and do something to change the situation. Finally, more effective teaching resulted when the content of the lectures was given a context that was highly relevant and useful to its members.

This entire case, however, also provides an example of the way in which interpretation, as we describe it, does not necessarily require a formally negotiated relationship. If a person can locate himself effectively in an unfamiliar or familiar place, interpretation can occur. There are times, however, when the interpretive stance, adopted formally in an invited, authorized consultancy, can effectively change not only individuals' functioning in their institutions but also what we might call "institutional self-awareness." We shall now examine one such occasion.

Part III

Applying the

Interpretive Stance

In this section we present two extended applications of the interpretive stance. The first involves the psychiatric unit in a large mental hospital where one of us (ERS) was the program director who invited the other co-author (AWC) to serve as a consultant to the program. The work that followed from this invitation, both by the consultant and by members of the organization, is described in chapters 8, 9, and 10. This personal account of the consultation illustrates how a study of people's experience in organizational roles can illuminate the organization itself. From the interpretive perspective, no role is insignificant; all roles capture a dynamic aspect of the task and a segment of the organization's overall functioning. From the initial consultative experience described in chapter 8, we developed a broader theory about dynamic functioning in organizations that is presented in chapter 9. Finally, chapter 10 describes how an internalized consultancy (first discussed in chapter 6 and illustrated in chapter 7 with respect to an individual) can be developed and used by an organization.

In chapter 11 we look at a second organization, a law firm, where we served as consultants and for which we designed a retreat. Here we focus on the use of negotiated interpretation and the development of a framework in which learning can occur. With such a jointly constructed interpretive framework, the organization can focus on its needs to attend to and define important shared values and beliefs.

8 ○ A Consultation to a

Unit in a Mental Hospital

Lhe Adolescent and Family Treatment and Study Center (AFTSC)
is a program within McLean Hospital, a 328-bed psychiatric hospital in Massachusetts. The program contains the Adolescent and
Family Treatment Unit (AFTU), a 12-bed unit for the inpatient treatment of severely disturbed adolescents, and provides research and training in adolescent psychiatry. The treatment includes individual therapy
for the adolescent and marital and family therapy for the adolescent's
family. The large interdisciplinary staff includes psychiatrists, psycholo-
gists, social workers, nurses, and mental health workers. Each of the
disciplines is responsible to its own department for professional issues
within the larger hospital but the interdisciplinary treatments are managed within the smaller AFTU. The individual therapist and the marital
therapist are co-therapists for the family work, and the nursing staff
coordinator works intensively with both the adolescent and the family
on helping to manage the adolescent's behavior. The family therapy is
conducted in front of a one-way mirror with staff observation when
possible, and efforts are made to integrate all aspects of the treatment,
including the staff's responses to it, in staff rounds. Once a week there is
a multiple family meeting for all families on the unit, including all siblings. In addition, the therapeutic milieu is designed to promote rehabilitation, and the unit offers a school program, an active rehabilitation
program, and numerous activities in which both parents and adolescents participate.

The need for consultation arose because of organizational problems that were perceived as arising from the existence of the program as a significant entity within the hospital. The growth of the program and the publications deriving from the unit's work had achieved recognition. This prominence, desirable as most felt it to be, seemed to be focused on the director; the staff did not feel they were benefiting from this recognition. Staff members felt isolated from one another and could not find a satisfactory way to collaborate, differentiate, and further develop the program's treatment, training, and research. Knowing of my (AWC) interest in organizations, the director invited me to examine and analyze the staff disarray.

THE EXPERIENCE OF CONSULTATION

Two aspects of the consultancy experience require attention: the response of the consultant entering the institution and the response of the staff. Initially I felt that I was being politely kept at a distance. Soon after my arrival it became clear that although the director believed he had authority to invite me on behalf of others, he was mistaken. Either he had assumed that he could do this without checking, or the participants, when they saw me arrive, withdrew any permission they had previously given. This appeared to be symptomatic of the director's isolation. Although he felt dependent on his staff for their work, they experienced neither his dependency on them nor their own connections to him in his role. I was introduced to the administrative staff group, which included the heads of the various disciplines in the program plus other senior level clinicians. We were able to discuss the situation as a group, and eventually a very loose contract was negotiated: I could talk to anyone in the unit who was willing to talk to me. But it was made clear that I was not expected to produce anything useful.

I soon discovered that the administrative staff group was something other than administrative: it, too, had no power to authorize me to consult with anyone or any group within the AFTSC. Each interview had to be specifically negotiated with the group or person involved. In some cases I felt I had to assert my authority to consult; in other cases the interviewees volunteered wide-ranging explorations of the significance of the program within the hospital, the world of mental health, and, finally, their own career and personal worlds.

Two major themes emerged from this early phase of the consultation. The first concerned authority: who could authorize whom? Could anyone, or any group, speak for the whole? People spoke freely about their "personal authority," but this seemed largely to disguise their perceived lack of place in the organizational structure. "I acted on my personal authority" somehow sounded more legitimate than "I did what I wanted," although it seemed to amount to the same thing. In effect, this need to exercise "personal authority" suggested that staff members were feeling organizationally disconnected from the director and that they, therefore, could not speak with the authority derived from his having delegated certain responsibilities to them.

The second theme concerned the remarkable intensity of the staff's commitment and their wish to belong to the program, to its ideas, and to one another as colleagues. Again, this appeared to be symptomatic of a failed negotiation of aspects of mutual dependency between the staff and the director. This expressed itself in an unusual way. Any consultant is accustomed to becoming a focus for dependency. Here, however, my experience was qualitatively different. In part because of my being both connected to the director (through his invitation to work and our personal relationship) and an outsider, staff members wanted to believe that I could at least stand up to him. And, in fact, their desire appeared to be that I could provide the missing connections between feelings and work. Though there was no possibility of my competing with him in the fields of treatment or research, staff members hoped that because of my outside role—and, perhaps, because of my role as a clergyman—I might be able to say some of the simple things that they felt unable to articulate. This was expressly stated in one meeting: the "Freudian stuff" could be left to him, but I might touch the "real, human experiences" of those working in the AFTU. In the minds of the staff, there seemed to be a separation between "feelings" and "work" that was symbolized by their efforts to get me to represent the former while the director stood for the latter.

The two issues that emerged in the earliest stages of this consultancy, then, concerned the structure of authority in the organization and the staff's unfulfilled wish to be connected to the director and to have him connected to them. In particular, the link between the institution's task and participants' feelings of belonging had become obscure. The lack of a firm connection came to be seen as the director's fault: he embodied the task, but in such a way that at least some of the staff had difficulty claiming it for themselves; on the other hand, he had founded the AFTSC, a worthwhile enterprise for which they felt affection and to which they were profoundly loyal.

As my work progressed, staff suspicion seemed to decline. People requested meetings with me; discussions ran over their allotted time; some asked for a second interview. My presence and the freedom that people in every role had to participate in the exercise in any way they chose seem to free them to talk to each other in unfamiliar ways. "Why couldn't we say that to each other before?" asked people in several meetings. Another group reported with surprise that a routine sharing of information had been performed with unaccustomed efficiency and clarity. Yet I had done nothing at this stage other than talk to people. Two specific experiences illuminate the value of these discussions.

I was made especially welcome by the nursing staff. Before our meeting, I had felt anxious about the lengthy time allotted; I could not imagine what we might discuss for so long a period. In fact the time was only just adequate. In addition, my discussion with the mental health workers turned out not to be just a series of complaints, as I had anticipated; instead they shared freely with me and with one another both complex experiences and interpretations of those experiences. Partly, of course, this may have been due to their hope that I might convey messages from those who, in their phrase, "stoke the furnace downstairs" to other parts of the system. But I felt that there was more to it than this. Because I was including them in the consultation, both in their own right as a group and as a subgroup of the nursing staff, and encouraging them explicitly to talk from their experiences in those roles, they saw that I valued them and their work.

In these conversations, I also received many personal confidences. Discussions about the working conditions of AFTSC suddenly shifted into revelations about intimate areas of individuals' private lives. Frustrations in living and questions of meaning, well beyond the presenting issues, were freely shared. It was as if most of those who worked with disturbed families and adolescents were lacking the opportunity to face their own disturbances in personal and family life. The outcome was greater personal disarray than seemed to be recognized by the senior administrative staff. Moreover, the way the program functioned (which attracted them to work in it) created demands that felt intolerable. As one person put it, "You can't say or do anything here without ending up on the [psychoanalytic] couch." There was confusion between what was inside the organization (essential data for the treatment program) and what belonged in each person's private world. Such confusion is undoubtedly endemic in this type of work, but opportunity for exploring it seemed limited. A person's "real, human world" seemed undervalued to the extent that it was always pulled into the "Freudian world" of the staff role. People consequently found it better to keep things to themselves.

THE ISSUES PRESENTED

As the consultation progressed, I began to get a sense of the institution of AFTSC "in the mind." This developing collaborative picture, discussed in Chapter 5, allows one to look at the organization as a whole in a way that transcends its parts.

The AFTSC is housed on the top two floors of a building. On the first of these floors are the patients' living quarters and the nurses' station; above are the therapists' offices and the administrative and therapy rooms. "Upstairs" and "downstairs" were constantly compared by the staff. This geography seemed to have become the formal expression of a series of fantasized polarities: you were either an upstairs or a downstairs person in the hierarchy; you were either invited by the director to contribute to decision making or uninvited; you were either in or out. Underlying these stereotyped complaints were serious questions, but these formulations provided secure areas in the mind to which the staff could revert as a defense against further stress, discussion, or probing. Again, this polarity appeared to capture a division in the institution between feelings (downstairs and devalued) and therapy "work" (upstairs and valued).

My own experience at the outset of the consultation vividly illustrates how I was captured in one of these polarities and how I used it for interpretation. The initial question was whether the staff would work with me as a consultant. Although the debate on this issue took place in my presence, I was clearly an outsider. However, once an agreement existed for me to do some sort of work—it was no more specific than that—I suddenly found myself "inside" very intimate, private areas of people's lives. It was not, therefore, simply a question of being in or out, but of being violently shifted between the two extremes, although at this stage the significance of the shift was unclear. Nevertheless here was the first piece of evidence: staff members' claims of being in or out led me to examine my own feelings concerning my role, raising significant questions about the organization. Why was there no negotiation around what was in or out? Why was this polarity so tightly held? And why was the switch across it so sudden? I suspected that this rapid shift might relate to the fact that the institution was not one in which mutual dependency was felt or acknowledged. This examination of the interaction between my feelings and those of the staff, elicited several pieces of evidence about "inside" and "outside" as metaphors about the organization itself.

1. The staff understood that they worked "inside" under personal stress that they inevitably took home "outside" with them after hours. The reverse, however, was being overlooked: namely, that they also brought with them into the unit certain pressures from home. The program was based on the theory that the total environment was involved in the patient's treatment. But in such a context, where was the place for friendship, attachment, and intimacy between staff members? And, where could staff members discuss the tensions in their own families that resonated with their work on the unit? More than one person spoke to me sadly of limitations and disappointments in relationships with colleagues in the program.

Because relationships were public both theoretically and practically (for example, the nurses and mental health workers had no private space in the building) and because every person's behavior was assumed to provide at least some evidence concerning the clinical treatment of patients, the one person who could be relied upon not to interpret—the program secretary—became the repository of personal confidences. Most of the therapists worked only part-time at the hospital and so could reorganize and distance themselves by working elsewhere in different environments. Full-time staff, essentially nurses and mental health workers, did not have that opportunity and were deprived of space and time for that process. They felt ignored and undervalued, claiming that their contribution could not be heard. Their inability or unwillingness to articulate their experiences resulted in a hidden exchange of feelings that was directly contrary to the ethos of the program and thus felt illegitimate.

2. Although it was not possible in this exercise to investigate AFTSC's place within the wider environment of the hospital, a boundary existed that affected everyone's work but that no one, except possibly the director, could address. Moreover, it appeared that the staff had not grasped its dependency on the director to do so. For example, the question of which patients to admit exposed differences in the assumptions of the staff of AFTSC ("inside") and the McLean hospital staff ("outside"). In addition, the larger hospital provided the nursing service and had different expectations of them than did unit administrators. The director's role with the hospital's nursing administration was unclearly negotiated, and the nursing staff seemed to become progressively less sure about which constituency (hospital or unit) they were dealing with and, more importantly, to which context their feelings should be related.

3. In a treatment program of this design a critical issue is "Who are the patients?" I began to envision two groups of patients: the proper patients, adolescents and families ("inside") and the staff ("outside"), who were being "treated" by the director and the psychiatrist. The range of hopes, fears, resentments, and cooperation that the "official" patients displayed was paralleled among the staff.

This affective process among the staff was usually discussed in terms of communication. General information seemed difficult to come by. As a result, two "interpretation-free zones" were created, places where relaxed and uncomplicated communication among the staff could be facilitated. One was the nurses' station on the bottom floor; the other was the secretary's desk at Reception on the upper floor. Such informal arrangements can be found in most organizations. Here, however, because of the all-inclusive theory of the treatment program, these zones were intrinsically illegitimate, even subversive. Their existence suggested that people were unsure about their roles within the organization and were therefore having difficulty finding appropriate means for sharing their feelings about these roles.

The picture that emerged of the organization began to help me interpret my original feeling of violent oscillation. "Inside" and "outside" appeared to be centrally important metaphors that related to other divisions in the institution, including downstairs/upstairs, devalued feelings/valued "work," hospital determined treatment/program values. These turned out to have structural meanings for the enterprise.

Two entities were intimately linked but were not being managed in relation to each other: the program and the individual. The AFTSC program expected the staff to have a shared attitude toward the treatment program and a commitment to the ideals of the program. But each individual staff member had his or her variable sense of connection to the whole. The individual's experience was of either having to submit to and incorporate an overwhelming and unclearly defined AFTSC package or to protect himself from it. This struggle was experienced between staff members in their formal work roles and staff members as individuals. In essence, there was a sense that staff members were being *instructed* to share their experiences—not that this was to be negotiated and that they could choose what was and was not to be shared. This lack of negotiation, it seemed, was at the heart of the failed mutual dependency between the director and the staff.

The lack of integration between individual experience and the organization's task and work roles represented one interpretation of the oscillation I had experienced in my own role. The theory on which the program's work was based, and to which the staff on the whole were highly committed, implied that these individual, internal struggles provided necessary data for grasping the experiences of patients in the treatment program. But in practice these experiences could not be examined because there were no limits to the exploration, and an unlimited exploration was too exposing for the staff. Since the staff felt that they could not halt an exploration once initiated, it was safer not to agree to start it at all.

To compensate, the staff created informal subgroups in which they could discuss their feelings about their feelings. These groups included the night nursing staff, the mental health workers and day nurses, those engaged in research, trainees, resident doctors, the director and psychiatrist, and an important "group of one"—the secretary. Some people were members of more than one group; other groups were unsure who their members were. But fundamentally it appeared that staff members used such personal connections as a means of trying to control the oscillation that each of them experienced between their individual person and the whole institution that they corporately formed.

Yet, although such behavior enabled individuals to survive psychologically, in the context of their work within the AFTSC this arrangement seemed disloyal. Each staff member, whatever his or her role, knew that the theoretical basis of AFTSC, which attracted them to join, involved thinking through the connections between the family as an organization and the individual patient in the role of family member. If the staff could not do this for themselves (in relation to the program as family and themselves as individuals in organizational roles), where were they to derive their authority to treat patients using this model? My assumption was that this dilemma reflected a managerial obstacle that might be clarified by examining the structures of the institution.

THE ORGANIZATION OF AFTSC AND ITS EFFECTS

The designation at the entrance to the building was "Adolescent and Family Treatment and Study Center." In practice, however, most of the activity and thinking occurred within the clinical treatment program, which was known as "The Adolescent and Family Treatment Unit." Treatment was the primary concern of the hospital and of the patients and their families. Distinguishing AFTSC and AFTU was sometimes difficult. From time to time, for example, reports were published under the heading AFTSC, although the content exclusively concerned the treatment program and its operation. People spoke of "the AFTU training program," although training was an identified function of AFTSC. These apparently pedantic points indicated an organizational dilemma: it was not possible for the staff of AFTSC or for those who worked exclusively within AFTU to speak coherently about their organization to an outsider. To the hospital administration the enterprise was AFTU, one treatment program among many. The staff needed to recognize this perception, since the hospital administration was dealing with their world on the basis of its perceptions, not theirs.

Two problems will highlight these divergent perceptions. First, although the unit had certain criteria for the patients who could be admitted because of the unique style of treatment, which was also the focus of the research interests of AFTSC, the hospital, which was concerned with overall admissions, could not accept these criteria. This led to inappropriate referrals and pressure about the number of patients. Uncomfortable disputes consequently arose, diverting energy, which was already limited by the demands of the program, from the task of patient treatment and leading to feelings of guilt and frustration.

The second problem involves those trainees who were psychiatric residents. These physicians were essential to the whole treatment program and their work was carefully integrated into it. The hospital made a policy decision to change the residents' rotations from a twelve-month to a four-month cycle, thus disrupting the treatment being offered in AFTU as well as the residents' own learning and research contributions to AFTSC. This decision generated anger toward uncomprehending hospital administrators.

Each of these everyday problems was to some extent created and to a large extent compounded by the unclear distinction between AFTSC and AFTU, as well as by the staff's inability to authorize and depend on the director. Given this internal confusion, the hospital authorities were understandably uncertain about what they were handling. The same was even more true for the staff at every level: they were unsure of their place within an apparently familiar environment, and so were not performing to their own satisfaction or to the level of competence required of them.

Confusion about tasks and authority is not unusual in any organization. But in AFTSC, since it was assumed that authority flowed only from the top down, voices from below could not possibly be heard. The mental health workers felt that they were at the end of the pipeline of authority and that ideas were shared with them only grudgingly and as a last resort. Key material for the treatment program, the sort of evidence on which its theoretical base depended, was being suppressed. For example, nursing staff members did not notify the director that a night staff member had visited a patient (who had experienced sexual abuse as a child) during the day, bringing a present. Role confusion also resulted. For instance, the director appointed the secretary to be program administrator and then assumed she was a member of the directorate (the director, the psychiatrist in charge, and the nursing supervisor); but the secretary was unclear about what her new duties were. Within AFTSC the key task of supervising research had been allocated to one man. But after a while he assumed that the director was performing this task while the director assumed that the arrangements remained as before, and the task essentially went unperformed. Not only were individuals not functioning at their best; the enterprise itself was not functioning according to its design.

A primary element in the treatment program was that the total environment in which the patients lived—the milieu—constituted "treatment." Patient care, therefore, was constantly being negotiated among staff, parents, and patients. But the nursing staff seemed to lack the authority to participate in this negotiation. In practice, most families dealt pragmatically with nurses and mental health workers, but neither group had any opportunities to discuss and shape the program's theoretical applications. They worked mostly in accordance with the policies of the hospital as a whole. Thus many of the nurses assumed that AFTU was no different from any of the other units: doctors treated and nurses did what they were told to do in their own idiosyncratic fashion.

An additional split was thus uncovered. Although at public meetings, research staff spoke of "the holding environment," different groups on the unit were working with different models of this environment. The therapists were working with a dynamic interpretive model constructed from the various interactive psychotherapies—individual, marital, and family. This was also the model that prevailed in published papers from AFTSC. In contrast, the nursing staff on AFTU managed a behavioral holding environment in which they housed and cared for the patients and at the same time dealt with behavioral aspects of the patients' and families' disorders that remained uncontained by the structured therapies.

The confusion and the difficulty in knowing what to do about it were directly related to the lack of organizational clarity between AFTSC and AFTU. AFTSC, the overall enterprise of which AFTU was a part, offered training and research. Yet training seemed restricted to official trainees, seminars and lectures were only available for outside groups, and research remained the prerogative of designated "researchers." If research were to be given priority as a task of AFTSC, one major consideration would be how the mental health workers on AFTU, who lived with the patients most of the time, might be assigned genuine roles in that research and how they themselves might also acquire training for their work with adolescents. This was only one example; similar considerations applied to all other staff members. In essence, the question was one of integration: how could the tasks of AFTSC be recognized and understood by all the staff so that AFTU, with all its roles, could be fully integrated within it?

THE SUGGESTIONS

Whenever pressures were felt within AFTU, all perception of the structure and significance of AFTSC tended to disappear as did the staff's recognition of the director's authority. Since the patients were disturbed adolescents, such pressures arose frequently, and thus the whole enterprise often seemed to be AFTU alone. In other words, training and research, the components that belonged to AFTSC and were represented by the director, vanished. This sense was compounded both from within and from without. Within the program, all staff gravitated toward their previous experiences or training in patient care when under stress, so that simple survival became their job criterion. From outside the program, McLean Hospital also assumed that the primary institution was the treatment unit. Once staff colluded with this assumption, by losing sight of AFTSC and its values, they felt deprived and behaved accordingly. They seemed to have lost the reason for being there in the first place. They began to feel (rightly) disappointed at their level of professional performance, but unclear why.

AFTSC had three major tasks that competed for primacy: treatment (in AFTU), research, and training. The first was being well managed, especially with the growth of the unit. The second was gaining in prominence, because it served the other two tasks. Quality research attracts trainees and gives the staff a sense that they are doing more than going through the therapeutic motions. And since on this unit trainees doubled as therapists, the more highly qualified and motivated they were, the more effective the treatment program would be. In AFTSC, the training task itself was confined to the trainees. The staff's learning needs, which must be considered in any negotiated interdependency, were not being addressed.

In addition, one crucial point was in danger of being overlooked: in a research organization rooted in an interactive treatment program, all participants contribute to the findings from their different perspectives. The question, therefore, was how the rest of the staff, in whom so much undisclosed data resided, might participate in the research.

The treatment program also needed one obvious issue to be clarified —who are the patients? Because the focus was family therapy, the staff thought of the families as the patients. In contrast, the families considered their hospitalized adolescent to be the patient. This produced uncertainty in the AFTU staff from time to time, with unpredictable effects. The organizational point was significant: there was no place where staff as a group could effectively address this question. Although the whole enterprise abounded in committees, meetings, and working groups, they had lost contact with tasks. People were left uncertain about their authority and the notion of the enterprise as a whole was located largely in the mind of the director.

When my experiences as a consultant and the staff's experiences were linked, we could develop a joint interpretation. My original experiences of authority confusion and rapid oscillation found an interpretive connection to the program's structures and to the staff's confusion concerning their tasks.

My final recommendations were designed to clarify the program's structures in relation to the tasks in such a way that every staff member could develop a sense of his or her appropriate responsibility for the future development of AFTSC as a whole, thus joining in a structured way the director's authority. This final section is abbreviated, but it illustrates how the consultation is brought to practical completion when tasks and roles are better defined. The later working of AFTSC and AFTU, which is discussed in the following two chapters, may then be read in context.

THE FINAL PROPOSALS

Connections between AFTU and AFTSC

The treatment task, embodied in AFTU, was to become more clearly the chief responsibility of the psychiatrist, who reported to the director of AFTSC. Nursing was to be provided by the hospital, which authorized the nursing supervisor to provide this service. The nursing supervisor was to provide nursing according to standards established by the hospital. The director of AFTSC was to authorize her to manage the milieu and its staffing. Other lesser responsibilities could be clarified, but essentially AFTU as a treatment program was to be the responsibility of both the psychiatrist and the nursing supervisor, each having clearly defined authority for different aspects of the treatment. Their joint connection to the director opened the possibility of a broader link between all staff members and the other two tasks the director represented: research and training. In addition, these two tasks were further clarified and expanded. With this broadened authorization and negotiated interdependency, the staff could develop further its delegated authority to manage those personal experiences that were relevant to the treatment.

Meetings

In a small institution where staff operate in multiple roles, meetings tend to proliferate in an attempt to help all to feel that they are contributing. The outcome, however, is generally frustrating and confusing. The failure to connect many of these meetings to the primary tasks represented by the director resulted in people feeling excluded. A simplified structure was therefore proposed.

Two structured meetings were proposed for AFTSC, a policy council and a management team. A policy council, to be chaired by the director, was proposed to advise the director on policy development, to monitor the workings of AFTSC, and to test these workings against stated policy. The membership would include the heads of the three activity systems of AFTSC—the director of treatment (the psychiatrist), the director of research, and the director of training—and one knowledgeable person from outside the unit, to keep the council from becoming insular. Other staff members would be invited to contribute according to the issue requiring attention. In addition, a management team was suggested to coordinate the day-to-day operation of the three subsystems of AFTSC (*not* AFTU). This group would consist of the director, the psychiatrist, the nursing supervisor, the program secretary (as administrator), the director of research, and the director of training. The membership would, through representation, allow all staff, in whatever role, to deepen their contacts with the tasks and values of the larger program. Although the membership of these two groups would overlap, the tasks would be significantly different.

Since AFTU was the most complex of the subsystems within AFTSC, it required a management group of those involved in its functioning. The task of the AFTU management group would be to monitor the work of AFTU, to advise the psychiatrist, and to ensure that those working in the various parts were able to contribute to the thinking of the unit and were kept informed about its activities and their contexts. The member-ship, therefore, would include representatives of the various aspects of treatment (for example, admissions; individual, marital, and family treat-ment; and aftercare).

The story of this consultation involving the AFTSC and the AFTU provides the background for the theoretical development and further practical outcome described in the next two chapters. By examining the organization using the interpretive stance, the staff grasped an organiza-tional dynamic that is fundamental to our argument about institutions in general in the contemporary world. They learned that their individual experiences could be related to their institutional roles in a way that illuminated their work in the organization. In essence, the consultation revealed to the staff their capacities and their authority to apply the interpretive stance to all roles in the institution.

9 ○ Coping with

Unbearable Feelings

The consultation described in chapter 8 led us to explore the link between the feelings experienced by hospital staff in their work roles and their feelings about the patients. In turn these connections led us to examine the decision to hospitalize itself. From this study we were able to develop a larger theory about the dynamic functioning of organizations.

The manifest reason for hospitalizing psychiatric patients involves someone's decision that they are in danger of committing suicide or homicide, or that they are unable to care for or manage themselves. From another perspective, hospitalization can be understood as a consequence of the inadequacies of the family, the community, or the therapist in managing the feelings generated by the patient's behavior and communications. In other words, a patient may be hospitalized primarily because people involved with him cannot stand their reactions to him and to his behavior. The institution, in this view, may be used by society as a place to lock away unacknowledged or uninterpreted problems of unbearable human responses to patients' psychopathology. In therapeutic relationships, where these issues are condensed, such responses are termed *countertransference*; we shall refer to this as the management of unbearable feelings about patients.

In the context of individual therapy, such feelings are private, often unconscious, and symbolically condensed in the mind of each therapist. As a result, if any examination of the phenomenon is confined to reports from the therapist, a range of potentially significant issues may remain hidden. For example, patients in outpatient treatment are ordinarily expected without discussion to manage their housing, clean their wastes, and take care of their personal safety. Few of these issues enter the therapy overtly except in derivative form. But all of these issues and reactions to them exist privately in the minds of both therapist and patient and may become manifest at times when hospitalization is considered.

In contrast, the psychiatric institution is public and can allow for wider exposure and interpretation of these interactive issues. In the institution, individuals and groups can find ways to protect themselves from the pressures of otherwise unbearable feelings. These defenses can range from restraining the patients to rotating shifts, administering medications, and engaging in collective denial. A range of professional and paraprofessional groups explicitly takes responsibility for those functions that the patient previously struggled to manage alone and silently outside. The existence of a diverse staff can provide a way for patients to project and displace feelings that may be otherwise unmanageable in intimate relationships, including the therapeutic relationship.

THE HOLDING ENVIRONMENT AND THERAPISTS' DISGUISED REACTIONS TO PATIENTS

In therapy, the terms *containment* and *holding* ordinarily refer to symbolic interpretive ways in which the therapist manages the patient's (and his) feelings (Winnicott 1960b; Modell 1985). For severely disturbed patients, where communication occurs indirectly, this symbolic holding function involves the therapist's capacity to acknowledge, bear, and translate into words the painful feelings the patient projects onto the therapist through a myriad of behavioral and nonverbal means.

Sustaining and interpreting intense reactions to patients can be difficult and exhausting work. Representing the human environment for some patients may be more than a therapist can bear. Therapists often turn to their colleagues and supervisors, the literature, and, occasionally, to gossip in order to manage the stress (Olenick 1980).

With severely disturbed borderline and psychotic patients, whose impulsivity may be dangerous, simply interpreting these emotional reactions may not provide sufficient safety for the patients to allow therapy to proceed and to enable the patients to learn about their impact on their human environment. A variety of additional resources, ranging from symbolic structures to actual holding or restraint, must therefore be provided to help these patients tolerate and understand the sum of their experience. The containment provided within the therapist-patient pair for less disturbed patients must now be assumed by others—doctors, nurses, administrators. With this expansion of the holding environment, otherwise covert aspects of the unbearable reactions between therapist and patient become exposed.

In a treatment unit, aspects of unbearable feelings that cannot be managed within the therapeutic pair are displaced into relationships with different groups of hospital staff, who are expected to contain them without interpretation. This containment, in which painful and significant aspects of the human experience remain unacknowledged and concealed, occurs at a price, a price paid by both patients and staff. Concealment is built into institutional structures, which the staff may use unwittingly as a defensive measure to disperse otherwise unbearable reactions to patients' pathology, thereby insuring that important and potentially interpretable data remain hidden.

IRRATIONALITY AND INSTITUTIONAL STRUCTURES

However rationally an institution may be structured, irrational pressures contribute significantly to its existence and functioning.[1] Irrational staff behavior in a mental institution can interfere with the task of patient treatment. Social systems themselves can function as a collective defense against anxiety (Jaques 1955). And there is a difference between the symbolic holding inherent in verbal interpretation by therapists and the physical holding sometimes provided by nursing staff.

Nursing and therapy staff serve as differentiated aspects of a total institutional provision of treatment for patients. Each group, therefore, must handle and interpret both patients' feelings and staff responses to those feelings. However, nursing and therapy staff have different functions with correspondingly distinctive modes of working. Effective interpretation of unbearable feelings requires a shared understanding of the treatment task and recognition that the entire institution is engaged in an interpretive task for which some common language is needed.

In addition, the institution is composed of more than the officially recognized groups of treatment professionals. Since all roles in the institution contribute to the task of providing a holding environment, a similar awareness of function and self-discipline is required of other groups, from mental health workers to maintenance people to secretaries. An awareness of feelings in role is required of individuals throughout the institution.

THE EFFECT OF DISGUISED REACTIONS—A CASE STUDY

One of the tasks of AFTSC, it will be recalled, was research, and the program's design offered an opportunity for close scrutiny of patient-therapist interaction within the treatment process. Staff members attempted to interpret their problematic reactions to patients in organized individual and group supervisory sessions as well as through observation and recording of family sessions. Staff interactions were also increasingly examined as a reflection of the dynamics existing between the adolescents and their families. But although the staff as a whole (both nursing and therapy) managed its work competently, both psychiatric and nursing leaders were concerned about the difficulties in developing and sustaining collaborative thinking in this large multidisciplinary staff.

As the consultation progressed, the interdisciplinary tensions in each treatment case on the unit began to emerge. Because the specific issues were comparable in every case reviewed, one case example will illustrate these tensions.

A fifteen-year-old adolescent girl with an eating disorder was hospitalized following a serious suicide attempt. Her mother suffered from a chronic disease that left her partially crippled. Not wanting to burden anyone, she kept her anger and sadness to herself, though these emotions were apparent in her behavior. She had become increasingly withdrawn and unavailable to her children and to her obsessive, isolated husband. When the patient was fourteen, her father became preoccupied with business concerns and was intermittently absent from the home. Her mother consequently had sudden and unexpected outbursts of rage, and the couple began to express mutual contempt and withdrawal. Because of chronic difficulties in the home, the patient persuaded a neighbor to appeal to a relative for foster care. As this option was being pursued, her parents had another serious fight, and the patient took an overdose of tranquilizers and was referred to McLean.

In the hospital, the nursing staff became immediately involved in the patient's bulimia, which she attempted to manage by vomiting in her room. Nursing staff and housekeepers cleaned up the vomit with the patient. The nurses and mental health workers were regularly provoked by the patient's initial seductive engagements, sudden contemptuous demands, rejections, and struggles around limits. On one occasion, she required physical restraints and the presence of hospital security officers who, as might be expected, discussed their affective experience of these encounters with security administration, not with the treatment team. In reaction to their own anger and frustration, the nursing coordinator and others on the nursing staff had, on occasion, sometimes withdrawn affectively from the patient. Though these intermittent withdrawals were not uncommon in a chaotic environment with disturbed adolescents, the intensity of individual withdrawals was often obscured for the treatment team by the rotating shifts, which left nursing staff members reporting secondhand on the experiences of others.

The patient's therapist, new to the program, managed his anxiety about his inexperience by only perfunctorily checking in with the nursing staff and offering them intellectualized formulations about the patient. He and the psychiatric administrative staff did not inquire about the patient's vomiting. The nursing coordinator felt snubbed by the therapist and, though she did not know him personally, managed her irritation at him by hypothesizing that he was uninterested in her work with the patient and that he was "arrogant and supercilious."

During therapy, the patient was largely silent, and on the unit she openly snubbed the therapist in front of the nursing staff. Irritated, he suggested to the patient that she was trying to embarrass him. When the patient reported the therapist's remarks to her nursing coordinator, the nurse responded in a dry and automatic manner, "You should talk with your therapist." Because of her own withdrawal from the therapist, the nurse could not help the patient to think through her response to him. Though the content of her words suggested the manifest image of a working pair to the patient, the underlying affective tone revealed to the patient their own unaddressed and unresolved argument.

The patient experienced these reactions from her therapist and nursing coordinator (the most important pair on the staff to her) as repetitions of her experiences with her parents (the distant obsessive father and the overwhelmed, angry, and withdrawn mother) and of their chronically unsettled argument. Without a framework for shared thinking about staff reactions, the patient's experience of a reenactment could not be perceived. Instead staff responses were sustained and individually managed by silent "personal" interpretations, leading to mutual alienation between members of subgroups and enactment of the patient's transference.

In addition, hostile and unexpressed personal conflicts among staff members were augmented by chronic feelings within the nursing staff of being ignored and unvalued by doctors. This second type of interpretation (that feelings of irritation stem from social-status conflicts) also served to remove feelings from the treatment context. Although the personal and the social-hierarchical interpretations might both have been valid responses to affective experience, they functioned chiefly to protect the self-esteem of the individual and could not be drawn upon interpretively to further treatment through cooperation across subgroups. Instead, these interpretations interfered with collaborative treatment.

In this case, the nurse-therapist pair, supported in part by the patient's behavior, by issues of role and status, as well as by personal concerns, were repeating key aspects of the parental response in their relationship to the patient. In addition, essential responses to the care of her body were managed in isolation by nurses, housekeepers, and security personnel. Without a way of examining these experiences in relation to the treatment task, the nurse-therapist pair could only experience their estrangement as a personality problem, not as a possible issue of dispersed and disguised countertransference. They could not find a way to collaborate in helping the patient to see her own responsibility for her transference withdrawal and anger. The therapy could not deepen.

For this patient, then, there was little interpretive integration between psychotherapy and nursing care—between the interpretive "holding" done in the various therapies and the actual behavioral holding done by the nursing staff, housekeepers, and security personnel. This was true despite the general recognition that hospitalized adolescents often communicate acute difficulties through behavior. The staff as a whole knew that the behavioral management provided by the nursing staff and others provided a concrete response to the patients' dependency and that many of these patients had not achieved the ability to articulate their feelings in words, hence the need for hospitalization. Treatment was focused on patient behavior; it did not fully address the staff's affective responses.

PERVASIVE COUNTERTRANSFERENCE IN THE STAFF

The program consultation, since it did not directly involve therapeutic or nursing professionalism, allowed the focus to remain on organizational and personal issues. The personal and emotional risks involved in this kind of behavioral care were examined. It became clear that the therapeutic and psychiatric administrative staff had defended themselves from recognizing that the nursing response could be understood as an aspect of the patients' transferences as well as an aspect of their administrative roles. Similarly, the nursing staff had been unwilling to see the connection between their management functions and the therapists' interpretive work. Each staff subgroup was having difficulty in experiencing itself as part of a larger whole, defined by a shared treatment task.

The disciplinary boundaries, reinforced by the dynamic of patients' provocative fantasies and behavior and the staff's unconscious reactions to them, had left each group working in its own language around specialized aspects of the patient's life. Though each problematic incident of nursing contact was presented and seemingly integrated in rounds discussions, complete integration remained the task of the director and psychiatrist; individuals with different roles had difficulty finding a language for the integrated function of the treatment team. Nursing reports were concrete, spare, and anonymous. Staff members could not acknowledge how shared affective experience in relation to patients crossed disciplines. Because the psychiatric perspective dominated and its technical language seemed exclusive, families, patients, and therapy staff persisted in believing that the core of the rehabilitative work, together with the genuine holding environment, was located in the various therapy settings. Within their own group, however, the nursing staff saw themselves as providing the essential containment. At the heart of the unit, then, were two institutions in the minds of the various staffs—nursing and therapy —each of which carried the projections and counterprojections of the other.

In addition to the projections coming from the staff, families and patients managed their own anxiety through projections onto the nursing staff (Shapiro and Kolb 1979). These projections are particularly powerful for those who are unprotected by a closed office, a fifty-minute hour, and a limited and well-defined task. If the need for multidisciplinary management of staff reactions goes unacknowledged, nursing departments and other unprotected subsystems may contain their unmanageable responses to such projections by developing structures that prevent their contact with patients from becoming too intimate—for example, by rotating shifts, changing tasks, changing jobs, and ritualizing activity (Menzies 1960).

Clearly the nurses and mental health workers were carrying affective burdens that they felt were personal and unaddressable using the sophisticated technical and conceptual tools that the therapy staff believed they had developed for working through their own unbearable reactions to patients. The consultation revealed the possibility that the therapy and administrative staffs were using the structures of the nursing department to keep their distance from the nurses and mental health workers and that they were managing their own anxieties about their work by joining the patients in projecting the cruder anxieties onto the nurses and nursing staff.

The nursing staff provided the focus for the infantile behavioral impulses of both families and their colleagues. They were chronically mistreated because of both groups' efforts to split the "mundane" custodial tasks from the "challenging" therapeutic ones. This split may have reflected potentially interpretable aspects of a maternal/paternal dissociation or efforts to split feelings from thinking. In any case, in the absence of a shared recognition that each subsystem forms part of a larger transference-countertransference dynamic, the danger was that patients and staff could begin to experience the therapies as dead and intellectualized and the milieu as passionate and unmanageable.

The consultation revealed the institutional contribution to the isolation experienced by the nursing staff. The therapists had closed offices, but the nurses and mental health workers had no private space on the unit and, because they lacked the authority to evaluate their experiences in relation to their task, no private space in their minds either. Apathy in the nursing staff, as a phenomenon of contained and introverted anger in response to institutional structures, had not been explored in a shared setting; its relevance to the therapeutic work of containing aspects of patients' feelings could not be identified.

RESOLVING THE COUNTERTRANSFERENCE

Prior to the consultation, it was possible to assume that transference and countertransference were technical issues that concerned therapists and patients alone and that stresses and tensions between hospital subgroups represented either personality issues or traditional behavior: "Doctors always devalue nurses." Yet, when the shared treatment task was defined and the institution examined as a whole, it became apparent that those unbearable feelings in the staff which revealed centrally important and interpretable aspects of patients' treatment could be exposed by examining all the relationships within the unit—patient/nurse; nurse/therapist; patient/therapist. Each interaction represented more disguised transference and countertransference than the participants realized. Encouraging everyone on the unit to participate in a collective staff interpretation of affective responses in relation to the treatment made it possible to place staff tensions in perspective. Staff members became less likely to be caught in unexamined reenactments of transference projections, and treatment became more effective.

For example, a mental health worker was assigned a nursing role with an adopted adolescent girl after another staff member had left the unit. He requested that he be assigned to a new patient because he felt that his patient was too closely involved with the previous staff member to become attached to him; he was irritated with the patient. With the new framework, he could use his own reactions to gain some understanding of the behavior of the adolescent's adoptive parents, who were angry at her attachment to her biological parents. This interpretation allowed him to work more effectively with his patient and with her parents' response to her.

What had been lacking was a conceptual framework within which endemic anxieties in the staff could be identified, differentiated, interpreted, and thus managed. As we pointed out in the last chapter, in the absence of an interpretive methodology, a previously unacknowledged subsystem for discharging emotions had been created by the staff. Since "interpretation" was experienced as something only therapists did and the concern was that therapists would "do it to them," the secretarial area had become a place for personal and affective exchanges that were spared interpretation: the "interpretation-free zone." This subsystem served as an important container for staff affects, with the secretary being experienced as a "universal aunt." Subsequent unexamined and uninterpreted pressures on her interfered with her work and led her back into the nursing station, where a similar zone was created. The nursing station became the ultimate point at which the secretary and others from the therapy staff discharged powerful emotions unconnected to the treatment task. Not only did this process function as a useful safety valve for the staff; it also, in effect, turned the nursing station into a waste container. As a consequence, important affective communications from patients to staff were merely discharged instead of being examined.

DEVELOPING THE INTERPRETIVE STANCE

If aspects of institutional irrationality stem from the staff's unbearable responses to the patients' chaotic needs, it is crucial for the task of treatment that a way of identifying and using these responses be found. A shared intrastaff interpretive stance is required to examine the staff's experiences of this irrationality in their institutional roles. Clearly, not all staff experiences or reactions require interpretation, but a stance for interpreting feelings that are related to the treatment of patients in which staff from every discipline can participate is essential.

Our framework for interpretation posits that those aspects of the patient's relationship to the individual therapist that prove unbearable are displaced onto staff in different roles. This displacement is inevitable, since symbolic holding through words alone is temporarily not possible for hospitalized patients. Interpretation then becomes the responsibility of the entire staff. As the patient becomes capable of translating feelings and behavior into words, the therapist can begin to interpret the displacements onto the staff and help the patient bring these feelings back into the relationship with the individual therapist and the family. The organization, therefore, needs to develop a straightforward, nontechnical language for articulating the staff's affective experience. The specialized psychiatric language may keep different staff groups from exploring these experiences, to the detriment of staff competence and effective treatment.

So, for example, in our case study of the patient with the eating disorder, as the nursing staff articulate their experiences of affective withdrawal from the patient's unpredictable seduction and contempt, the therapeutic team can recognize this as a re-creation of the patient's difficult relationship with her mother. Similarly, the difficulties between nurse and therapist can be recognized, in part, as an unwitting re-creation of the parental discord that contributed to the patient's isolation. As the staff begins to understand the significance of these reactions, they can be less caught up in them, thus freeing the patient from an unproductive repetition and enabling the therapist to more easily interpret these reactions and integrate them into the patient's treatment.

There are a number of criteria for developing the interpretive stance in a mental institution. First, there must be some protection of the individual staff member's experience, so that not everything is presented for group interpretation. On the adolescent unit, this is managed by providing supervision within each discipline to help define the limits of applicable experience and by organizing specific meetings at which shared interpretation is collaboratively developed. Caution in determining desirable modes of understanding in a psychoanalytically oriented treatment unit is vital for patient care. If everything is liable to be interpreted at any time, patients as well as staff will have no secure or private areas for themselves. Such vulnerability produces potentially disorienting uncertainty. An organizational culture has to be developed in which interpretation is encouraged within clear limits. Such a culture is created in part through the director's authorization. In a chaotic environment, a clearly defined culture can protect personal privacy and give staff members the freedom to articulate job-related affective experience without feeling that they need to expose all of their lives. The creation of such a culture also sensitizes the staff to the prevalence of countertransference issues in general and trains them to identify these issues in themselves and others. When each staff member informs himself or herself by asking the essential question that marks the interpretive stance—"What is happening to me in my role, and why?"—and then invites and participates in collaborative attempts to interpret role-related experience, a fundamental focus for institutional development is created. With such a stance, important aspects of the inevitable staff disputes become accessible for shared clarification, interpretation, and use in furthering the task of the unit —the treatment of patients.

Second, there must be an organizing framework. Theoretically, this framework is the treatment task, which includes efforts to understand the relationship between the staff's experience and that of the patients. Often, however, because of pressures from the wider hospital environment, professional rivalries, lack of resources, and the like, this primary treatment task may be transmuted into a financial or regulatory task (keeping the beds filled, managing competent medical records), and thus lost. Alternatively, sustaining the primacy of the treatment task might be relegated to those most in danger of working in isolation—the director or consultant, on the one hand, or the nursing staff, on the other. Both responses are defensive attempts to protect both staff and patients from the stresses of genuinely examining patients' feelings and unbearable staff responses to them. Keeping the primary focus on a treatment-oriented interpretation of affective experience requires everyone's continual oversight.

Third, the stance requires the development of self-reflection. In order for this model to function effectively, each staff member must act as a consultant to himself or herself to determine which aspects of his or her affective life to bring into the work. The interpretive stance acknowledges external pressures on the institution, the individual psychopathologies of the staff, and the authority issues endemic to any organization. Some of these factors may require shared interpretation, others need only internal recognition. The decision and the responsibility rest with each staff member. In practical terms this means that hypotheses concerning the meaning of these experiences for patients' treatment are collectively generated by the treatment team and tested against the full range of experience and feelings within given roles. All hypotheses necessarily remain open to the scrutiny of others, not because of their status or expertise but because of the validity of their experience within their specific roles.

The interpretive stance also has consequences for organizational structure and style. In order for this stance to develop, those in formal authority roles (director, supervisor) must learn to recognize and respect the difference between their organizational authority and the authority of a person speaking from his or her experience in role. Organizational leaders who acknowledge this task-related authority support the continuing development of self-scrutiny among the staff.

10 ○ The Unit's Use of

the Interpretive Stance

The discovery of the relationship between unbearable feelings and work of the institution was only one outcome of the external consultation to AFTSC. Staff members' recognition of their own capacities to develop negotiated interpretations linking their internal experiences with the unit's work helped a different work culture to develop. In other words, the organization internalized the interpretive stance. Interpretation became a more reliable method of addressing the tensions of working life, serving both the task and the needs of members.

This development came about in part because of personnel changes in AFTSC. How well AFTSC had internalized the interpretive stance became clear after three key people—the psychiatrist, the clinical nursing supervisor, and the rehabilitation therapist—departed from the unit. The new psychiatrist found herself struggling with her new role. She had been in training at AFTSC during the consultation and had witnessed the organizational changes that occurred as a consequence. In her new job, she found herself unable to overcome the resistance she was encountering from the staff and unable to link, organize, and integrate the staff around the clinical task. Though she found her supervisory meetings with the director helpful personally, she felt that larger organizational dynamics were interfering with the collaborative work. She therefore asked the director to consult with her staff.

Given the involvement of the staff with the previous consultation, the request was not surprising. But this time the request came from someone other than the director. A member of staff used her own authority and her own experience of confusion to invite consultation. In effect, she was asking for assistance in her own struggle to incorporate the interpretive stance in her role. In so doing she was, possibly unwittingly but nevertheless effectively, supporting the interpretive culture of the AFTSC.

The psychiatrist's request and the actual consultative process were an expression of the stance the staff had adopted as their mode of working. That the psychiatrist invited her immediate superior to work directly with *her* staff in the consultative role is itself evidence that the unit was imbued with this stance. The specific problems were presented in terms of her difficulty in making sense of the changes on the unit as the staff struggled to come to terms with a new chief psychiatrist, nursing supervisor, and rehabilitation therapist and their way of working together. The request, therefore, was for help in developing a collaborative staff interpretation of the changes.

THE BACKGROUND

In my role as director of AFTSC, I (ERS) was relieved to be invited into AFTU to consult. I had been worried about the problems of staff collaboration in this complex program but wary about interfering with the psychiatrist's authority by intervening. I had uncomfortably settled for limited management from a distance, by working through the psychiatrist and through my supervisory interventions with other senior staff. This compromise was affected by the general level of competitiveness and anxiety about authority and power relations among and between disciplines in the hospital as a whole.

The unit was undergoing a major transition in personnel. I knew that at times of turmoil groups often develop dependent wishes for powerful intervention from people in authority. The director's authority, however, is derived not only from formal authorization but also from his representing (and articulating) the task of the program and the vision behind it to which the staff can commit themselves (Menninger 1985, p. 339). In this instance I felt that the psychiatrist was experiencing a lack of this authority during the transition.

Although I was physically present and, so far as I (and others) could perceive, had lost none of my authority or my clarity about the task, the psychiatrist felt that she could not find in her working role the authority from the director—me—that she felt she needed. In particular, she could not seem to articulate an interpretation of the current difficulties that took into account the dynamics of the transition and at the same time provided a link to the larger task definition of the unit. Case conferences, supervision, and management-group meetings provided opportunities for the staff to be in direct contact with the director, but these seemed to be insufficient. As a result, the staff were experiencing difficulty finding their own authority for acting in their different roles in relation to the program's task. As head of the unit, the psychiatrist represented this problem and presented it for consultation.

Although this dilemma might possibly have simply reflected the staff's difficulty in working with a new person and the new psychiatrist might have brought in the director to help the staff deal with morale, commitment, and motivation problems, I did not feel that she was abdicating her responsibility. Had it been an abdication, my agreeing to function as consultant might have served as an unconscious collusion with the psychiatrist and the staff to obliterate her role and replace her with the more familiar and reliable director. This would have been a defensive use of the interpretive stance.[1] But I did not think this was the case.

When I began to meet with the various individuals and groups, my experience as a consultant was strikingly similar to that of my coauthor (AWC) several years before—people were eager to join in a discussion and to authorize me in the consultant's role. Though they were at first intimidated because I was the director, they quickly accepted my consultative function and offered their own interpretations. This willingness to join in suggested that the psychiatrist was right in inviting and authorizing the consultation and that the notion of interpretation as a working stance had to be renegotiated and reinternalized, given the new leaders.

THE DATA PRESENTED

The psychiatrist, representing the treatment task, was clear about her need for consultation. She could not grasp her managerial role and found herself stuck in the more limited and familiar role of "physician." She was preoccupied with issues of patient and staff safety, overinvolved with the nursing staff, overwhelmed by details of the individual cases, and missing a sense of the whole. Despite the director's efforts to clarify the situation in supervision, she could not seem to formulate a clear view of the various subgroups she was supposed to manage or, more importantly, of how these groups should be working together. She and the nursing supervisor could not resolve their differences regarding the roles of head of nursing and head of the unit, and she needed help in addressing her experience of being left with too much to manage.

The earlier consultation had revealed that unmanaged feelings were often projected onto the nursing staff. Now they found themselves searching anew for their authority. They, too, had a number of new staff members, including a new nursing supervisor, and they initially had difficulty in authorizing me to consult. They appeared preoccupied with the power of my director's role and impatient for me to use it to order people to work better. However, once the new nursing supervisor understood my desire to work with the nursing staff to achieve a negotiated interpretation, she was able to authorize the consultation and to participate fully.

In their discussions, the nursing staff focused on the difficulties involved in the transition to a new nursing supervisor and a new psychiatrist. Questions were raised about tradition: Are old ideas valued? That is, can I still use the interpretive stance? If so, with whom does it need to be renegotiated? Are there any new ideas? How do new ideas relate to valued traditions? Although there was much talk about "new ideas," I could not get any precise sense of what these were. They seemed to be a series of generalizations about being more or less restrictive with the patients. There was a split in the nursing staff, with the more experienced staff holding to the notion of working with the patients as a group, whereas newer staff focused on the need to pay attention to individuals. I found myself thinking about the older "group" who had previously developed a way of working together and the difficulties of incorporating the "new" individuals into the staff.

The secretary, as we have noted, was informally expected to manage many of the staff's unexpressed feelings and consequently carried a great deal of pressure to connect various aspects of the unit's work both managerially and interpretively. During the stress of transition this demand inevitably increased. It emerged that she felt authorized to occupy this complex but essential role on the basis of her residual sense of authorization from the last psychiatrist. She had not made a working connection with the new leaders, since they could not find a way to use her information interpretively. So although practical issues could be managed, interpretations about feelings across staff groups could not.

The therapy staff took longer than any other group to decide to meet with me. They were impatient with the psychiatrist and wanted her to get on with her work; they felt they had no issues requiring consultation. They were, however, prepared to meet with me if it would help her. Though the psychiatrist related to this group in her mind as an integrated task group, they did not experience themselves as such. They had not previously met separately from the staff as a whole. This group is itself composed of a series of subgroups. On the one hand, therapists come from several disciplines—medicine, psychology, social work. On the other, the therapy staff included both senior staff and trainees. The consultation began to focus around the trainees.

On the unit, the head of the multidisciplinary team for each patient was the individual therapist, as interpreter of the individual transference. The people who occupied this role were trainees. Senior staff were therapists for the parents. A trainee and a senior staff member worked together in each family therapy. When the therapy group finally decided that there were issues that might be discussed with me, they focused on this collaboration. The senior staff were worried about the difficulties they were experiencing in exercising authority on the teams. The teams were headed by inexperienced people who, they felt, did not understand the work in sufficient depth. Their advanced experience was not being used, and they felt constrained in using it.

I was impressed with the ability of the entire staff to be open with me in the meetings. The staff discussed their anger and disappointment with the work and with the program without feeling intimidated because I was the director, perhaps due to their experience with the earlier consultation. They accepted my consultative role which, through the psychiatrist, *they* had authorized. Though I remained in this role in my meetings with all subgroups, as I listened to their discussions I began to see myself in my director's role reflected in the material from each group. Gradually, I began to hear many of the complaints and concerns expressed by each group also as criticisms and interpretations being offered to me in my primary role of director. Each theme raised for me the question, "How do I know about that in my role as director?" So, for example, when nurses discussed the tension between old and new ideas, I thought about my own tension and resistance about integrating my own "old" formulations with the ideas of the new staff. When the senior staff therapists discussed their feelings of constraint with trainees, I heard echoes of my own constraint in exercising my authority with the new leaders.

In my final meeting with the therapy staff, they overtly raised the role of the director for discussion. The therapists felt the director should be someone who "keeps his head, while all those about him are losing theirs."[2] He should provide a context where work can take place. Anxieties included whether the director should function in so many roles and whether, as a consequence, he might "lose his head" with disastrous results. Here again, I listened to the connections. Just as I could hear the staff's criticisms of each other also as criticisms of the director, I began

to hear their concerns about the director also as comments on his dele-
gations of authority to them. I began to worry about the difficulties they
were having in keeping their own heads. What had I done with my dele-
gations of authority and how had I managed the boundaries between
groups?

The trainees had specific concerns. They felt the program had too
many trainees. There were not enough cases; it was too hard to get into
the system; there was not enough attention focused on their learning
needs. They acknowledged their own reluctance to participate in offered
learning opportunities. They felt that the nursing staff required too much
of them. For instance, the nursing supervisor asked them to help new
nursing staff members to learn their role when they themselves were not
sure of their own. Their experience was similar to the psychiatrist's in
that they were confused about what administrative duties were expected
of them and where they were to learn about these tasks. They were thus
caught between the nursing supervisor and the psychiatrist and, as trainees, felt unprotected and vulnerable to displaced anxieties from each
and from both.

My final meetings were with the administrative staff group that has
overall responsibility for managing the unit. These meetings exposed
some of the organizational confusion within AFTU: although this group
represents all the other subgroups on the unit and has a managerial role,
the psychiatrist did not think to negotiate my consultation with it. And,
as director, I had failed to advise her to do so. My conclusion was that as
director I had not fully authorized this group through the psychiatrist,
and that I therefore was using this group unwittingly for some purpose
other than shared management. Seeing this problem allowed me to begin
to grasp my contribution as director to the psychiatrist's sense of having
too much to manage, which had given rise to the consultation request.

As well as I could tell from the one meeting, the covert task of the
administrative group had been to contain and manage the dependency
needs of the staff, not to accomplish work. I wondered whether this
group's containment of dependency reflected their unaddressed mutual
dependency with the director. The group spent its time comforting the
new psychiatrist and nursing supervisor as they tried to carry out their
excessively heavy managerial burdens. The group did not collectively
recognize that its job was to manage overall treatment, together with the
teams. They could not seem to accept that several independent task
oriented groups (administration, rehabilitation, therapy, admissions
could each contribute to resolving the daily problems of managing th

unit. Interestingly, the therapists' representative in the administrative group—one of the most experienced therapists on the unit—felt inhibited about speaking because of his doubts that he alone could represent the complexity of the therapy group. And the secretary, who manages most of the connections between the various groups, was largely ignored in the meeting. I began to suspect that I had not fully recognized my task as director to renegotiate the authority of the other disciplines during this transition. As a consequence, the new psychiatrist was overburdened and the collaborative work of the unit was suffering.

Data from other meetings with the rehabilitation therapist, the school teachers, behavioral therapists, and the admissions social worker corroborated this picture.

INTERNALIZED CONSULTANCY AT WORK

This consultation provided an example of an institution as a whole employing the internalized interpretive stance. Ordinarily, consultants are outsiders. They are invited to associate with the institution for a period of time and to embody the interpretive stance. By working together, client and consultant can discover the task around which to join and so negotiate an interpretation of the organization. However competent the consultants may be, they are protected to a degree from intragroup tensions by their distance from the dynamics of the institution. The first consultation presented in chapter 8 was an example of an outside consultant.

However, when an institution assumes interpretation as its basic stance, an important shift occurs. Now interpretation provides the context for confronting problems. On behalf of the staff, the psychiatrist found this approach in herself and articulated it. And, although acting as consultant, the director also found himself consulting to himself in that role. In other words, the unit as a whole discovered that its members were engaged in mutual consultancy, which was effective because the notion of the interpretive stance itself provided a specific protective boundary for work.

There are, we would argue, occasions when an internal consultant is the only one who can do the job. In this case, the role of director was central. This role is a critical one with a high profile; for the outside world, the director represents the institution, and for the inside (institutional) world, he represents the task. The real work of this consultation occurred when the person at the heart of the institution—the director—learned about the disconnections between the disciplines and thus recognized that the interpretive stance had to be renegotiated with the new leaders. The consultation, therefore, was a function of the institution, not of the consultant or client alone. This explains how subgroups of staff within the institution could serve as consultants to the director at the same time that he (in his role as consultant) consulted with them.

Dr. Carr's consultation clarified the institution's self-awareness and helped the participants feel more comfortable in assuming differentiated roles. When individuals in central roles left the organization, the self-awareness remained, but disarray ensued. The staff was lost in the familiar place of its own adopted working stance. It then moved to recover that stance by practicing what it preached. By inviting someone to represent consultancy, the members—and hence the unit as a whole—could more rapidly recognize shared assumptions, note issues that did not at this point need to be addressed, and come to a negotiated perception and interpretation of the key issues at the moment.

INTERPRETATIONS

When a person is working in a series of roles and one becomes primary, the others are not laid aside and cannot be ignored. In this case I did not cease to be director while also being consultant; I worked from my several experiences, trying to gain the distant perspective of the consultant without denying my intimate knowledge of the unit and the personnel, many of whom I had appointed.

In the earlier consultation, three tasks had been identified that vied for primacy—treatment, research, and training. The request for the present consultation seemed to derive from the treatment task, since the psychiatrist, who was in charge of that task, expressed her anxieties about it and her role. But the evidence showed that the psychiatrist in fact functioned as a representative of the broader institution (AFTSC) and that the staff's concerns involved the third task—training. The idea of learning became predominant, whether that of new staff, of those designated "trainees," or of the director. Because this task was one that belonged to the whole enterprise and not just to those called trainees, the consultation touched upon the program as a whole, the level of its performance of other tasks, and consequently upon people's roles.

In this consultation, we began to recognize that internal consultancy essentially involves mutual training and learning. Because the tasks of treatment and research had been previously explored, training suddenly appeared to be not a third task competing for primacy with the other two but rather the basic culture of the unit—the air we breathed. One pays attention to air only when it changes.

The central question of the consultation was how people could feel supported in their own stressful work when those upon whom they relied for guidance and advice were dependent on them for *their* learning. At this time of transition, when new managers quite publicly had to learn, their capacities to delegate genuine authority were inevitably limited. As a consequence people occupying central roles in the treatment program had to rely to a greater degree on themselves and on the sense of the task that they had inherited and could sustain. When problems arose, as was inevitable, especially in a pressured clinical system, one unconscious result was to resent anyone's need for learning, including one's own. This resentment made it difficult to join anyone else in learning. Yet when a major change occurs, all become learners in this new system, including the director. Intellectually it is possible to admit that change provides creative opportunities; emotionally, however, members of an organization may become too angry about their unmet dependency needs and too divided to take advantage of these opportunities. When anger sets in, engagement in collaborative learning stops, leading to feelings of being stifled, bored, burned out, and unvalued. In this instance, the sense of being unvalued and stifled not surprisingly manifested itself chiefly in and around those designated as trainees. Their difficulty in protecting themselves from the demands of the nursing staff seemed to be a direct result of these pressures.

Since devaluation of learning was the issue underlying the staff's difficulties in collaborating with a new administrative team, the beginning of the solution was partially addressed by the consultation itself. The way the psychiatrist invoked the interpretive stance by inviting specific consultation provided an unintrusive pathway for all to reorient themselves toward the cooperative interpretive stance for which the unit stood. This consultation heightened the staff's awareness of their roles in relation to the training task and its organizational consequences.

One further important point emerged that has broader application for both treatment and training. There was usually a delay in acknowledging people's strengths in the unit. The trainees, for example, were qualified, skilled people whose assets were underestimated. And, although the rehabilitation therapist had the specific assignment of seeking the patients' strengths and capitalizing on them, the staff had taken a long time to take advantage of her skills. Further, as I discovered in the consultation, there was a tendency to see the need for learning as a weakness in colleagues rather than as an opportunity and a shared task. When these observations were linked, we were able to see that the patients were themselves in a sense undergoing training and that there was a connection between the assumptions being made about professional training and those being made about the treatment of patients. In other words, the patients' needs to learn were also being devalued and seen as a weakness, not as a potential asset. Again, therefore, an issue manifested in one system—training—was symptomatic of a problem in another —treatment. If the internalized interpretive stance had not been applied and made explicit in a specific consultation, these connections would probably not have been so fully noticed and addressed.

11 ○ Values and Beliefs

within a Law Firm

The consultations discussed so far focused on specific organizational dilemmas. This chapter describes a consultation that explicitly addresses issues of belief and values. We have touched briefly on these in discussing the hospital, especially in so far as the staff developed their own sense of valuing the experience of working from an interpretive stance. In this example, however, values and beliefs become the central focus of interpretation.

Questions of value, meaning, and belief seem inevitably to arise when the profoundly intimate yet ordinarily hidden connections between diverse people are exposed for examination (Miller 1980). These questions seem to pull us beyond the range of what is ordinarily accessible in people's current experience. But we consider it a distinctive aspect of our approach to interpretation that these factors are included rather than dismissed. We may be uncomfortable with them, but we cannot ignore them. We wish, therefore, to demonstrate how values and beliefs might be addressed without losing sight of the working task.

In this consultation, a negotiated interpretation of the organization emerged from our collaborative efforts to sustain a self-reflective stance. We were able to make inferences and develop connections between our differing experiences in our consultative roles that allowed us to address the larger concerns of the organization.

THE INTERPRETIVE FRAMEWORK

As we have described earlier, consultants do not simply observe people's behavior and comment on it, instead they reflect on their internal experiences to create hypotheses about the current activity of the group as a whole. Consultants have authority to the extent that they are right—that is, when the interpretation drawn from within so resonates with the feelings of the group that the members have to acknowledge and deepen it. In other words, such interpretation begins from experience in role, but can extend in its effect far beyond.

When consultants are working from an interpretive stance, their interpretations are primarily based on reactions to them and on their internal responses to those reactions. Thus interpretive work originates in transference and countertransference and is rooted in the theory and practice of psychoanalysis.[1] As they begin to integrate these experiences, consultants generate a series of interpretations at different levels. The consultative task requires paying attention to others' experiences, so that interpretations can be joined and deepened. In our earlier discussion of the hospital treatment program, we noted that those engaged in collaborative interpretation needed some secure place—an "interpretation-free zone"—within which to protect themselves from having to interpret every feeling and experience. Not everything must be spoken, but it is useful if what is spoken can be heard.

The setting developed by Freud for carrying out psychoanalysis (the couch, the two-person encounter, the analyst's relative reserve) has its own distinctive constraints and boundaries. For instance, the internal experiences of both patient and analyst are related to the relationship between the two and interpretations are generated about that. The setting itself provides a structure beyond the individual, where projections can be contained and interpreted.

A consultant working with a group or organization must also address internal data. But at the same time he is required to structure a framework that enables others to recognize and use one or more of the levels of interpretation. Whereas the analytic setting is relatively simple in structure, the setting for work within an organization is not. Nothing is excluded, and as a result consultants work not only with their own feelings but also with the need to create a setting in which interpretation can be heard.

CASE STUDY: THE FIRST RETREAT

Able Bingstrom and Cabot[2] was a two-year-old New York law firm with twenty-five lawyers. The executive committee of the firm originally requested consultation and the development of a weekend retreat for the partners because of a vague sense of disquiet about "interpersonal issues." I (ERS) was hired and met with the executive committee. From this meeting it appeared to me that the partners were presenting what they experienced as personal distress to someone who was believed to be an expert in that field—a therapist. But their interpersonal tensions were not separable from the context of their work. Hired, therefore, because of my therapeutic background, I had to expand my involvement, without denying my role as a therapist. Similarly, the members of the executive committee found themselves presenting personal feelings on behalf of all the partners of the firm. Therefore, they had to attend to their roles in relation to the firm and to the executive task of handling the firm's problems of perceived "interpersonal issues." Thus from the beginning both parties—the executive committee and I—were engaged in simultaneous negotiation with each other and within ourselves. This was the first step in a negotiated interpretation.

Their recounting of the firm's history made it clear that once the firm's survival had been dealt with, other important concerns were beginning to emerge: what the firm would stand for, how it would represent itself to the outside world, how it would grow, and how individuals and subgroups within the firm could find a voice in the firm's management.

At the initial retreat, it emerged that an atmosphere of mistrust permeated the firm as a consequence of an unconscious avoidance of the competition and differentiation that had arisen when the three senior partners had united to form the firm. These unaddressed anxieties had been condensed into an administrative structure designed not to foster a supportive work environment but rather to present a facade of unity. One senior partner had been made managing partner; the other two controlled and limited his work, rather than supporting it. I explored with them the illusion of equality inherent in the term *partnership*, suggesting that necessary differentiation was being experienced as dangerous. The partners decided to authorize the managing partner to act on behalf of others (while remaining clearly accountable to the partnership for his actions) and to form a policy committee and a practice management committee.

THE SECOND RETREAT

One year later, I was asked to organize a second retreat to focus on tensions between partners and associates (junior lawyers without tenure). There were now fewer complaints about the managing partner, but the competitive tension within the firm seemed to have shifted to the level of the associates. These men and women were feeling unvalued, finding their professional development as lawyers difficult within this organizational context, and not feeling fully connected to the firm. They did not receive organized feedback about the quality of their work, and no clear policy described how the associates were to be evaluated or whether they had a future in the firm. As a consequence, they felt misused, exploited, undervalued, undertrained, uninvited to share in the firm's development, and left to develop secret personal relationships with various partners. Associates denied any competition among themselves, though they were quick to report covert competition among the partners.

The practice management committee, which had been created to address such grievances, found itself without sufficient authority to do so. This committee included representatives of associates, partners, and administrators within the firm. Therefore, this committee reflected the dynamic themes within the firm, including the partners' lack of clarity about how to relate to associates. In particular, there was a disconnection between issues of practical management (notably finances) and the development of shared values. The firm seemed to have developed structurally since the last retreat and to be prepared to consider its future, especially as represented by the associates. After discussions with members of the firm, I suggested the following formulation as a basis from which to start to work:

> You are facing an intensely competitive legal world in New York in which several medium-sized firms have failed. Your original commitments to each other to limit your size also limit your opportunities for development and growth. How is it possible, then, for this relatively young firm to bring management and values, issues of quality and commitment, experience and inexperience, partners and associates together into an organization in which all participants will feel connected to the joint task of personal, professional, and organizational growth?

As I reviewed the design for this second retreat, I decided that th presence of a colleague could be beneficial. Although he was not presen during the first retreat, my coauthor (AWC) had advised me on some possible ways of getting at and behind the presenting issues. We had also reviewed the retreat afterwards. I therefore arranged with the partners for both of us to attend the retreat. At the retreat, then, the participants were invited to work with a pair of professionals: one of us (ERS) could be viewed as the "partner" (having already established personal and working links with members of the firm) and one of us (AWC) as the "associate" (someone foreign to and unknown by the participants and hired by the "partner"). This parallel structure offered opportunities for significant dynamic interchange.

In the opening Friday evening meeting, we reviewed the first retreat, the previous meetings with subgroups, the decision to include a colleague in the consultation, disquieting personal communications from individual partners (without revealing the details), and especially the sudden and shocking illness of one of the senior partners. We suggested that all members of the firm might be feeling concern and confusion about these events. In addition, although individuals might easily get lost in the seeming anonymity of "The Partnership," "The Associates," or "The Firm," the illness of the senior partner emphasized the importance of individuals in the firm's life.

When the group as a whole tried to describe what they wished to examine on the retreat, the ideas that emerged were vague, unfocused, and unclear. So we asked the participants to begin working as individuals, briefly writing down their ideas about the future of the firm and their concerns, anonymously and privately. We collected the papers and ended the session.

Their responses were overwhelming. We were stunned by the intensity of people's worries about the firm as a whole and their care for and anger with one another as members of it. People were strikingly more forthcoming as individuals than they had been in the general discussion. We also received a number of technical descriptions of the firm and its work, whose accuracy we could not check, since we had little objective data available. The reports were filled with gloomy predictions about the firm from partners and associates alike. In addition, however, some statements praised the firm as unique in terms of the intimacy of the partners and its areas of specialization in the world of law firms and contained optimistic ideas about what it might stand for.

We adopted our interpretive stance as best we could and began to discuss these findings. We noted that because we represented a partner and an associate we had an opportunity to study our own interactions as a way of examining the dynamics of the organization. Although we were colleagues in our work elsewhere, we were not at this moment equal in terms of our involvement with the firm. Gradually this distinctiveness began to enhance our effectiveness. As we explored our competition in response to the need to make sense of the data received, we became differentiated. In a seeming role reversal, the one of us who was the "associate" became organized, rational, and managerial, whereas the one of us who was the "partner" became emotional, fanciful, and creative. Together, we might develop something coherent; separately, we were ineffective.

As the two of us struggled to interpret the messages we had received and to discern the connections to the organizational dynamics, we found ourselves unable to interpret our own feelings of desolation. This, as well as our lack of engagement with, and possibly flight from, the members, suggested that denial was a prevalent defense in the firm and that we were being asked to articulate a powerful dynamic. A series of images began to emerge from our discussion as we tried to create an exercise for the members that would allow them to engage with the overwhelming concerns they had experienced. Every image involved disaster—being on a sinking ship, traveling in the Arctic and confronting death, running an emergency ward and handling the problem of triage, living in South Africa and facing political disaster, and removing a crippled spaceship from earth orbit without further endangering the crew.

Finally, with this last image, we recognized that we, too, were beyond our own orbit, that we were developing increasingly regressive images about disaster, and that we needed to face the unsettling reactions the firm was creating within us. Three options were open to us: to reduce the affective differences between us ("Yes, you're right"); to adopt a professional defense ("Let's devise a structured program for them tomorrow"); or to rationalize away our feelings ("Maybe we're just tired"). We recognized, however, that we were together in a profound regression. Consequently, adopting any of these solutions would have constituted a flight from something painful within us and, presumably, something difficult to address within the firm. Our interpretation was that our anxiety about our own survival as consultants suggested that the question of the firm's survival was the unacknowledged theme of the retreat. The tension between partners and associates was a first-level defense against their shared anxiety about and inability to face the future.

After this initial regression, we began to reflect on what was happening to us in terms of the task of the retreat. From our experience o interpreting our own regression, we realized that an issue as frightening as survival might possibly emerge through a similar regression and an attempt to interpret that experience. We therefore considered how to structure such an opportunity for the participants, thus providing the framework for a negotiated interpretation involving both content (the issue of survival) and the process of discovering it (contained regression). We needed to provide the participants with a hypothesis with which they could work.

INVITING AN INTERPRETIVE STANCE

The next morning, we offered our stark hypothesis with evidence derived from the data offered in the retreat so far: You are all, with your different roles and responsibilities, worried that the firm may not survive.

We pointed out, among other things, that more than half of the members had explicitly raised this question and that the size of the firm seemed problematic. Given partners' commitments, the firm could only grow so much. As a result, the associates experienced their request for evaluation and feedback from the partners as a life or death request. Partners and their particular associates constituted a series of competitive groups that shifted and regrouped, producing tension between collaboration and competition. All were dependent on those partners who brought in business, but on whom were those partners dependent? The individual, whatever his or her position, had to ask, "What does survival demand of me?" It was in this context that questions were raised about whether the survival of the organization was to be at all costs or on the basis of some distinctive value or set of values for which the firm would stand and be known. Loyalty and commitment were both required and offered, but to what? In spite of superficial protestations, it turned out that the bottom line for commercial survival—money—was not in fact enough. If survival anxiety is not addressed, it often becomes focused on making money, but loyalty and commitment cannot be located there. Issues of beliefs and values—particularly integrity, training the next generation, and excellence—though not usually discussed openly between partners or associates, emerged as crucial for the firm's survival.

The participants' neither immediately denied nor accepted our hypothesis. Instead, they began to work with it and with the evidence, relating it to the experiences of individuals and of subgroups. One partner even linked the discussion about not valuing the associates to his dream the previous night about children dying. It therefore seemed to us that our hypothesis was reasonable.

We now had to structure a process to enable the participants to experience sufficient regression to be able to collaborate with us in producing a more refined working interpretation about the firm. Freeing the members from any need to discuss the hypothesis, we divided them randomly into two groups and explicitly invited them to abandon words, consciously to return to a childlike mode of communication, and to draw a picture with crayons of a medium-sized law firm which, in their view, could survive. We suggested that they use all their professional skills to face realities about the firm.

We remained available for consultation as they worked. One incident from the exercise illuminates the significance of the learning process. Two members, one from each group, approached us separately. One came to check the precise boundaries of the task. The other, the managing partner, came in a jocular mood to invite us to join his group so that we could "learn something." In seemed to us that the firm, through these two requests, was offering back to us a version of our own earlier experience. The first asked a rationalizing question, the second fancifully invited fusion (encouraging us to lose our consultative roles and join them). In their struggle, they had come up with regressive defenses that were similar to ours. Recognizing these defenses was a key step toward their negotiated interpretation of the major issues facing the firm.

NEGOTIATING AN INTERPRETATION

The pictures drawn were interesting and usable in discerning blind spots and shared values for which the firm could stand. They graphically displayed the interdependence between partners and clients, the competition within the firm, and tensions about "the bottom line." For our present purposes, however, the regressive process of the collaborative work is more significant, since interpretation emerges from process. In this case the parallel configuration of the consultancy (a partner and an associate working with partners and associates) was central. In the first place this provided the firm with a simple and usable opportunity for projection. This was all the more important with a group such as this. Unlike therapists, lawyers are not generally accustomed to recognizing or naming this dynamic process of projection, regression, and learning. Although it could have been described by us, the discussion would then have remained largely intellectual. Our configuration assisted the clients in unconsciously recognizing an aspect of their lives—their differentiation, competition, and collaboration—with which they were experientially familiar but which they could not articulate. The first condition, therefore, of negotiated interpretation—providing a usable context—was provided. We should also note, however, that our configuration into partner and associate, which was task related, benefited us as well as the clients, for it allowed us speedier access through identification to the underlying issues to be addressed.

Interpretation is not the same as understanding. A negotiated interpretation provides an opportunity for learning. Change in an organization, of whatever sort, is itself a form of learning. In this instance, the retreat offered both an occasion for consultation about a problematic issue and a clear learning opportunity for the institution as a whole and for its members. Learning always involves some regression. But if the regressive feelings that emerged in us, for instance, had simply been described as such and allowed to run free, they would merely have been interesting. They might even have been destructive, particularly if we had simply launched a hypothesis derived from them onto a tightly controlled and rational group of lawyers. Certainly they would not have been useful. If feelings are to be used as interpretive data, they need a holding context within which they can be managed. The notion of task—in this case, the shared focus on the relatedness between partners and associates—provided that context.

THE ROLE OF THE CONSULTANT

In dealings with a client of any type, consultants represent the task of learning. By using their feelings in their roles as consultants, they affirm the legitimacy of the regression that accompanies learning. In a sophisticated organization, the importance of such regression can rarely be acknowledged. The presence of childlike or unconstrained feelings in adults often evokes embarrassment. Yet without these feelings, learning (that is, change and development) cannot take place. By applying their regression to the prevailing task, consultants create both a model of interpretation and a setting in which it can be attempted.

In this case we saw how, by structuring an event that took advantage of both the members' data and the experiences the two of us had undergone, we were able to invite the clients to make similar use publicly of their feelings and dreams. They thus began to discover the problem that they had hitherto denied and began to propose ways of dealing with it.

We did not offer any particular organizational suggestions. The partners and associates together, through their regression and joining, discovered their connectedness to each other and the ways in which their interpersonal and intergroup tension represented unaddressed conflict within the firm as a whole about values. Uncovered through the pictures drawn and the collaborative discussion, these included: commitment to the future, learning, risk taking, and specialization. These were articulated in our presence and further developed into management proposals after the retreat, including clarification and organization of the evaluation process for associates, modification of the associates' roles, and attention to the values articulated by partners in the recruitment process.

A crucial aspect of the consultant's role is managing the process of interpretation. In this case the consultants experienced a rapid and turbulent regression. The dramatic nature of this experience facilitated our formulation of a working hypothesis for this firm. But, as we have argued, consultants, whether in a group or in an organization, are always immersed in transference and countertransference. Because they are consciously trying to address and employ their empathic feelings in relation to these projections, they will inevitably regress much faster than the clients will. Failure to recognize this difference may sometimes account for people's bewilderment in response to what feels like premature interpretation. Sometimes, because they have not yet found their own regressive place, clients become unable to join the consultant in collaborative interpretation.

This style of interpretation, however, is marked not so much by what the consultant may offer to the client as the extent to which the process facilitates the clients' discovery that they have the interpretation themselves. In other words, the consultant, by enabling this regressive learning process to occur, affirms an interpretive stance and its use.

Two points are especially worth noting. First, consultants, in affirming the interpretive stance and, as far as they can, enabling its adoption, also represent its inevitable incompleteness. Having reached one level of interpretation, it is their role to indicate that this level cannot be the end but is only a step to the next question. In the case of any institution, a consultant's work with it will constantly refocus attention from the addressed boundary to the unaddressed. Logically, therefore, for any organization the question of its relatedness to its broader context inevitably arises. What is more, the idea of regression as an inevitable institutional phenomenon and the recognition of the need for its management and interpretation may provide a theoretical handle by which to link the individual, the organization, and society. As we have seen, through a managed regression within an interpretive framework, individuals can discover their connections both to each other and to the contexts within which they work and live.

Second, this interpretive approach is not value free. The lawyers, like the hospital staff, discovered that values and beliefs are not peripheral to the membership of their respective organizations. When the interpretive stance is employed, these connections become more evident. The consultants always help clarify these connections, for even if the links are not obvious, the consultants recognize that people are nevertheless profoundly interdependent. And by simply working together, both client and consultant are implicitly affirming such connections between people as a primary value to which they are deeply committed.

Part IV

Developing Wider

Interpretations

Throughout this book we have explored the links between individual experience and institutional behavior, and we have tried to show that the contemporary experience of being lost in familiar places does not imply that men and women can do nothing other than acknowledge this feeling. By employing the interpretive stance, we may discover new and useful ways of living in and working with the large institutions that dominate our social and political lives.

We have already shifted from viewing the individual alone to considering the individual in the context of the group or organization and the group within its environment. Individuals function on behalf of one another, sometimes consciously but more often unwittingly. Similarly, as we have seen both within the family and within organizations, groups function for one another. Here, we extrapolate one degree further to ponder the notion of "environment." This leads us to consider how organizations themselves might function on behalf of one another within those vast, largely undefinable, but powerfully effective worlds of "society" or "the nation."

This is an exciting area to contemplate, but one fraught with difficulty (Miller 1980; Khaleelee and Miller 1985). When we become aware of the group, our sense of the complexity of the individual and his or her behavior increases. When we add imponderables like "society" or "the nation" and the generalized dynamics that such notions represent, our range of awareness is further enlarged. This ever larger setting makes interpretation and communication more difficult because it introduces another major variable into an already extensive set—culture.

Yet we cannot deal with human behavior and organizations, the differences between individuals and groups, and the benefits to be derived from accepting and using these differences without acknowledging the influence of culture. Culture itself is ineffable. It is a collective phenomenon; its traces cannot be fully detected within the individual. It is, therefore, impossible to comprehend the individual data and find a suitable interpretive stance, not least because the grounds on which interpretation could be negotiated cannot be found. But using experience and observation, it is possible to reflect on the cultural dimension of individual and corporate behavior.

We have chosen to focus on two larger cultural concerns. The first is religion, for it is both a universal phenomenon and a highly personal one that addresses the question of what it means to have a role simply as a human being. Any reflection on religious behavior brings us up against symbols and ritual and questions of meaning, all of which are relevant for members of most organizations. We shall explore the cultural significance of religion through a case study and then present a more general theory concerning the functional significance of religion. Our second cultural focus concerns the central issue of developing an interpreted connection to others using the range of roles that are demanded of us—that is, finding an answer to the question, "How can I use my various roles to find my place as a citizen in my society?"

12 ○ Organizations

as Symbols:

A Study of a Church

We began this book with two major aims: to describe an approach that would enable individuals to find their way through the confusions of contemporary social life and to offer an explanation of how institutions can generate some coherence within society. But once we speak of "society," we begin to address feelings and other data too vast to be manageable in terms of our interpretive stance. That stance requires the linking of internal experience in role with external evidence in relation to a larger task. We do not lack internal experience in social roles. But what would constitute external evidence in society at large? And what could be the larger task? These data would inevitably seem to be less accessible than, say, evidence about a hospital or a law firm and clarity about their respective tasks.

If we are to carry our argument into the broader scope of the relationships among the individual, institutions, and society, we need an access point around which we can construct interpretive hypotheses. Certain social institutions would seem to provide such an access point. Definitions of their tasks can be problematic, but they are at least more accessible than the generalized notion of society. One such social institution is religion, which manifests itself not only in individual belief but also in organizations, such as churches.

The task of a church may seem far removed from that of a hospital or law firm. Hospitals receive patients whom they must treat and discharge; lawyers must attract clients, whose interests they must successfully pursue. A church has no such obvious flow of clients and consequently no immediately apparent task. Yet, the study of a church provides a useful introduction to our wider discussion of individual, institution, and society. For if we can discern a generalized task for such a familiar institution, we may be able to extrapolate to more generalized tasks that all organizations perform, perhaps unwittingly, on behalf of people in society.

Understanding this case study requires a little background knowledge of the church involved—the Church of England. The key terms used (and defined in the footnote) are *vicar, congregation,* and *parish.*[1]

THE BACKGROUND AND THE DISPUTE

St. George's Church stands in the suburbs of a large city. The area was first developed just prior to the Second World War, and there is no room for further expansion. Jews, many of them descendants of refugees who fled to England from Russia and Germany earlier in the century, form one major group within the parish. Some are retired and others commute to and from the city. They still own a few of the local shops, although many have now been taken over by a newer group of immigrants, Indians and Pakistanis. These immigrants arrived about a generation ago and, like their Jewish predecessors, prospered and moved out of the inner city. There are also some indigenous British people. Each of these three groupings—Jewish, Asian, and indigenous British—is clearly identifiable, although none is wholly confined to a geographical area. There are no ghettos.

The church building was erected in the 1930s. Most of the money was raised locally by the vicar at the time. Christian churches are customarily dedicated to saints. This one was dedicated to St. George, the patron saint of England. The church flag is the English national flag.

An important element in the parish is the number of schools, which are attended by a mixture of Jewish, Christian, Hindu, and Sikh children. There is frequent but courteous controversy over school holidays, which are based on the Christian calendar. Both the Jewish and Asian groups occasionally attract neo-Nazi hostility. But between the local multiracial inhabitants and the church there is largely a sense of goodwill. For example, they perform small mutual favors and publicly recognize each other's existence. Shops, for example, will advertise church events, and various sections of the community use the church hall on social occasions.

The congregation is a combination of those whose families originally helped build the church and others who are members of the minority Christian population living in the parish. The worship is ritualistic; that is, the priest has a prominent role, and bells, incense, music, icons, and images are used in the services. The church thus follows a style of worship derived from the Roman Catholic tradition. This is not unusual in the Church of England, but it is noticeable. The congregation is not inclined to extreme behavior or violent emotion.

Against this background of a fairly typical English parish we can examine the significance of a remarkable occasion of irrational behavior within the congregation.

A parishioner donated a statue of the Virgin Mary and the vicar had it installed, thinking it a desirable adornment for the building. The church's religious practices routinely included devotion to Mary and there was nothing to which the members of the congregation could have been expected to take exception. The vicar was, therefore, unprepared for the outburst that followed. The church wardens (the chief elected lay members of the church) became severely upset about the statue; the church council (an elected body of lay people) voiced resentful anger at the vicar; individual members threatened to withdraw their financial and emotional support. But no one could say precisely why he or she was so furious. The vicar was told that he should not have accepted the gift, that he should not have placed it in the church, that it was "not the right thing for us." Yet until that moment, the congregation had generally deferred to the vicar, following his lead in most matters, and they had been restrained and polite when discussing church affairs. The vicar could not understand why in this instance a kind of collective madness seemed to have possessed otherwise ordinary people.

Such disputes are not uncommon among people who are connected with one another through shared belief and deep personal commitment. Indeed, churches are especially prone to such episodes. So the vicar, an experienced person, initially treated this outburst as a temporary disagreement that would have no long-term consequences. But contrary to his expectations, the irrational feelings did not subside. On an earlier occasion I (AWC) had studied the local schools in this emerging multicultural area with a colleague who is a sociologist. This study had helped the vicar, who was involved in several schools, to clarify his role. I had also previously consulted with him and his church council about the church's task in that changing parish. Faced with this curious instance of incomprehensible behavior in the congregation, he again invited me to assist him.

APPLYING THE INTERPRETIVE STANCE

The interpretive stance is applicable even in such a diffuse and imprecise situation. On this occasion the vicar could find no connection between his feelings and the violent feelings of others in the church. He could find in himself neither anger nor defensive withdrawal. He was simply mystified. My first thought, therefore, was that he was denying some feeling in himself, perhaps about the statue, which was emerging in the congregation. But this idea led nowhere. He was rational in his role; the members of the congregation appeared remarkably irrational in theirs.

The interpretive stance requires us to relate internal experience in a role to external data derived from a task. In this case, there was no shortage of internal experience. What was missing, however, was a broader awareness of what might constitute external data and a clearer notion of a task. In this case, the roles of vicar and congregation within the church itself did not clarify the experience of conflict.

Partly as a result of having studied the schools and partly because the hypotheses we had developed about hidden tensions between the vicar and the congregation had led nowhere, the vicar and I began to look beyond the presenting behavior. I asked what this experience might indicate about the congregation's dynamic relationship to the wider environment. To do this we had to reflect further on the religious (that is, also cultural) factors involved. We suspended our thinking about this specific Christian church and tried to inquire where in ourselves (particularly in the vicar as a local religious functionary) similarly irrational religious feelings might be located. In other words, we consciously shifted the context from the local Christian church (the vicar and congregation) to the religious institution (the community church) and its religious-cultural environment. Thus, by using the interpretive stance internally to enlarge our perspective, we were able to consider the possibility that we were attempting to relate our data to the wrong context.

The context within which we could discover in ourselves related anxiety and irrational feelings about religion was the larger community. These feelings, derived from our experiences both within the schools and in the church, revolved around issues that were ethnic, cultural, and only secondarily religious. This parish (the geographic area containing the various ethnic and religious groups for which the church believed it held some spiritual responsibility) was suffused with anxieties about religious and national identity, values and beliefs that resonated within both of us.

The first set of immigrants (the Jews) had been concerned about how they would be received and had avoided having too high a public profile. They had grown more confident, however, and now openly identified themselves as Jews. Now the new Asian immigrants were the ones unnerved by life in an alien culture. Like their predecessors, they clung to their ethnic and cultural identity by privately affirming their distinctive religion. Their arrival, however, had revived in the parish fears similar to those earlier evoked by the Jewish immigrants. The occasional anti-Semitism and overt racism of the National Front (a small but vociferous neo-Nazi group) was one manifestation of these social dynamics. Nevertheless, whenever such attacks occurred, the general local response was mystification—"Why here?"

Under the surface of this outwardly integrated community lay unacknowledged and unresolved tensions. To put it another way, under the rational exterior of the different groups in the neighborhood there lurked powerful irrational feelings. The church was not the sole repository for these feelings; they also appeared in the schools. Under the guise of a reasoned discussion, quite irrational proposals were being made—different terms should be used for different ethnic or religious groups, holidays should be given for religious festivals, all languages should be taught to all children, and so on. The schools provided each group with a public and reasonably safe forum in which the struggles around national and religious identity could be legitimately waged in a changing community. But the deeper irrational aspects remained hidden.

Since the church (through its congregation and vicar) contributed to the local community, it was intimately involved in both the overt and covert dynamics. On the surface, its contribution seemed small. The majority of the population was clearly not Christian and the congregation was not outstandingly active. Yet, through a study of the vicar's experience in his roles, we began to discern a possible link between the manifest anxieties about religion and race within the two "immigrant" blocks of the population and the irrational reaction to the statue that had erupted inside the church.

Within the community, the church represented the nation to which the immigrants had come and to which they now belonged because it was the Church of *England* and because it was dedicated to St. George of England. By positioning the church within this broader context, I was able to assist the vicar in rediscovering a role he had already found was expected of him in the schools, where he was invited by virtue of his being "the vicar" to be one of the managers. In that setting, he was treated not so much as a Christian minister but more as a figurehead, whose presence provided enough stability so that different factions could express their opinions without drifting into a fight. By linking the mystifying behavior within the church to the vicar's experience of his symbolic role in the community, we began to develop an interpretation. We speculated that the church itself—like the vicar—had a role within the community as a whole. Two major immigrant groups (old and new) provided the focal points for powerful and irrational feelings about race and religion. These feelings had the potential to destroy all attempts to create a new community. Some structure had to be found to contain these feelings so that they were not let loose. And this structure seemed to be the local church which, unknown to its members, acquired this role because of its richness as a symbol.

Although the congregation erupted into irrational activity when the statue was installed, the emotions of the community as a whole appeared to remain orderly, and the community's goodwill toward the church and the vicar persisted. Indeed, apart from the internal dissension among church members, the picture remained one of cooperation, mutual respect, and genuine attempts among the different groups to build a harmonious community.

As we considered this dichotomy, we recognized that two of the groups concerned—Jews and Asians—were customarily among the first victims of prejudice. They also publicly combined their religious and their national identity and used them as vehicles for each other, as did, in some ways, the two of us English priests in our formal commitment to a national religion.

We could now begin to discern a connection between the outburst within the church and what was happening outside it. The congregation's irrational reaction had occurred because of a change at a key point of its distinctively religious life—devotion to Mary. We considered that this reaction might reflect a projection of disturbing aspects within the religious and national life of the two immigrant groups with which they had not yet come to terms. But this interpretation of what was happening in the church was not yet complete. Religious groups that were struggling with their identifications (as was apparent within the schools) might possibly project aspects of their disarray into an available, established, and seemingly secure religious body. But there was no obvious reason why they should. Perhaps in this case we were dealing with even larger, almost communal dynamics.

Religion offers one means of managing the irrational, frightening, and threatening dimension of life. Jews, Sikhs, and Hindus alike had been presenting their religious faith as a stable aspect of their lives that enabled them to sustain order within their separate ethnic groups. But in the unsettled conditions in which they now found themselves, organized religious activity alone may not have provided an adequate outlet for their irrational feelings. We hypothesized that the most publicly available alternative religious organization, one that was not in competition with them, was consequently being used for this function.

This interpretation was based on a range of evidence. Some was derived from the vicar's experience in the schools. There he represented, among other things, the idea of English tolerance, thus freeing ethnically and religiously defined groups to debate the meaning of membership in the community. The church, too, as was clear from its friendly interaction with local groups, was acknowledged as an entity of believed value in the creation of that tolerant community. By virtue of its dedication to St. George—its quintessential Englishness—it could sustain this ideal for the two immigrant groups. This tolerance, however, as exposed by the neo-Nazi use of Englishness as a racial category, was less secure than all might have wished.

These external dynamics, with which the church interacted and to which it contributed, then seem to have emerged powerfully within its own walls. The acceptance of the statue seems to have symbolized the acceptance of something new, at a time of unacknowledged general anxiety about newness in the community. It also stood for something "un-English" (devotion to the Virgin Mary, although part of the church's usual life, is associated more with the Roman Catholic than with the English church). Our hypothesis, therefore, was that what would usually not have worried the church members in their role as congregation had in fact impinged powerfully upon them in their roles as members of the community, as citizens. In that role, other groups within the community saw them as symbolically representing Englishness (especially tolerance). We suspected that their tolerance of differences in the community could be sustained because of the reliable sameness they experienced within the church. The episode of the statue had consequently thrown them into unaccustomed disarray and produced irrational behavior because the foreignness previously confined to the community had entered their private bastion. The vicar was protected from experiencing this sense of invasion because he had been unable, prior to the consultation, to connect the role required of him publicly (for example, in the schools) with his role as minister to this particular congregation. When the connection was made and interpreted, however, he was able to recapture the tensions within himself, and the discussion could be broadened.

UNDERSTANDING THE LARGER CONTEXT

This story illustrates the importance of discerning the dynamic context in which feelings are generated. Sometimes this context may be larger than is immediately apparent. These events occurred as old anxieties about racial identity and security were resurfacing. The underlying issue, however, was how to provide adequate security so that the different groups could engage creatively with each other around questions of their distinctive survival within the setting of community living. The Jews and Sikhs and Hindus had originally come to Great Britain because this security was available: they were all refugees from some form of intolerance. They now depended upon an ideal of tolerance symbolized by the notion of England. This local church made a symbolic statement about that ideal. The different groups were, of course, not obliged to focus their dependency needs on the church, but it was probably too convenient to be overlooked. Church members, however, were naturally unaware of this underlying dependency and their role in it. Preoccupied with their own activity, they could not perceive that their religious life might have functions for others.

We have already seen, in our study of the mental hospital, how a social system may provide a defense for individuals against threatening anxiety. We suggest that social institutions may function in a similar way. In this case we have studied an institution which, though small, had a significant role within the larger sphere of social dynamics. There remains, however, a major dilemma: What can one do with a hypothesis about the cultural use of a religious institution to manage social anxiety? Our hypothesis is drawn on an extraordinarily large scale. Is it of more than idle interest? Indeed, we may even wonder to what extent such a hypothesis could be thought of as "negotiated," since the discussion of it was largely confined to the church groups.

Our hypothesis exposed one of the church's tasks—possibly even a generalized primary task for religious institutions. Our notion was that one task of this church was to contain irrationality and dependency on behalf of the larger community. Through the episode of the statue and its interpretation, the church rediscovered this task.

Clearly, if our interpretation is correct, the church was receiving massive projections from the community. There was little or no likelihood of

our identifying these projections and offering them back to their origi-
nators. This is one of the problematic facets of life in any institution,
conceived in relation to other major contexts such as society. But because
projections cannot effectively be managed between one institution and
another, it does not follow that their being perceived is useless. In this
instance three positive outcomes can be immediately discerned. The condensed feelings that focused so painfully in the church exposed, when
interpreted, a wider perspective for the church's activity.

First, the vicar and congregation together became wiser about their
role within their wider community. Once before the church had recognized that its life and the lives of those around it were connected. That
was two generations earlier, when the church was being built, and before
the multicultural community had come to be. By interpreting the experience with the statue the congregation again became aware of the complexity of levels at which the church as a symbol might function. This
realization led the church as an institution to reconsider its tasks, and it
eventually restructured some of its internal organization to that end.

Second, church members became more critical about their faith. In
other words, that which sustained them in the church in the first place
—what we might in this context call their motivation—became less
casual and assumed.

Finally, the nature of church members' connections with each other
—their association—became clearer. This issue forms a key link to our
next chapter. In most organizations, as we have seen in the hospital and
the law firm, goals direct people's activity. From time to time a crisis
emerges. Sometimes with the assistance of consultants, the underlying
task is clarified, and members are able to discover or rediscover their
roles. But there is also an associative side of an organization, its human
or sentient dimension. This is the aspect of organizational life we touched
upon when we discussed the motivation and morale of hospital staff and
the central motivating power of values and beliefs in the law firm. In
many organizations, the associative aspect is secondary, but in some
institutions this human aspect is far more dominant.

A church's task is not always as simple to discern as that of some
other organizations. Because there is no overt task around which to
draw people together, bringing people together is itself the predominant
aspect of the organization's life. Such associative bodies, therefore, are
more acutely sensitive and susceptible to human irrationality and dependency (Reed 1978; Carr 1985b, 1985b). For this congregation, their
profoundly irrational reaction alerted them to the fact that irrationality

and dependency are never far below the surface in a church. They thus discovered an undervalued aspect of their existence as church members.

There remains, however, the question of how, if at all, this interpretation could be said to have been negotiated. The key boundary exposed by this case study was not simply between the church and the community. That distinction camouflaged the underlying boundary between rationality and irrationality captured in real and symbolic roles. The interpretation, therefore, was negotiated within the self, by examining experience in contrasting roles. The members of the congregation were individually and collectively also members of the community. The initial confusion of both congregation and vicar resulted from their inability to begin to see that they represented for others a number of things simultaneously—England, tolerance, Christianity, foreignness, and so on. Once they recognized these symbolic roles, a negotiated interpretation could be undertaken by the vicar and the members of the church. Without the broader societal context against which to attempt interpretation, these symbolic roles remained ungraspable and uninterpretable.

Those aspects of culture and society that impinge on such institutions are most accessible to those in positions of leadership, who are at the boundary between the organization and the outside world. In that position, leaders can generate hypotheses that can be offered back to members of the organization and tested against the data of individual experience in various organizational roles. Then members of the institution can arrive at a negotiated reality about the connections between their institutions and the world around them.

13 ○ Irrationality

and Dependency:

A Method for Survival

Every organization has its specific task. But organizations may also perform other, less obvious tasks within a society. We have already touched on Bion's speculations that social institutions might be managing large-scale, unconscious dynamics (see chapter 5). The aggression between nations, for instance, seems to be as much commercial as military (Kennedy 1988), for nations, through their commercial organizations, compete to gain a larger number of export orders. One generalized social task of industry and other commercial enterprises may be to carry out the fight/flight dynamic on behalf of the whole society.

A hypothesis such as this, one drawn on such a broad scale, can aid us in examining the internal workings of an organization. We saw an instance of this in our discussion of a local church. But even when an organization—for example, a law firm—has a more overt task, such a perspective is valuable. In that firm, the external competitive environment affected its internal workings. For example, partners and associates felt competitive with each other but were uncertain why. Alongside this struggle ran another one—less obvious but no less real—about beliefs and values: in the turbulent world of commerce, what values can be relied upon? We may put this in another way: as the partners and associates dealt with the fight/flight dynamic of achievement, how was their dependency to be dealt with? The question of what people find reliable and confirming—what they believe in—is an aspect of the dynamic of dependency. In the law firm, as partners' and associates' competitiveness became more prominent, issues of dependency emerged as well.

This interpenetration of basic human group dynamics forms the basis of our argument in these last two chapters about the individual, social institutions, and society. Here we begin to go somewhat beyond the interpretation of personal experience characteristic of the interpretive stance into broader speculation. The object is to provide a framework for such speculation within which the interpretive stance can be employed. We shall approach this exploration of the larger social tasks of institutions by considering religious institutions, for they seem to expose the boundary between people's unconscious needs, particularly the connections between dependency and irrationality.

As we saw in the opening chapters, the conflict between dependence and autonomy lies at the heart of our experience of the family, the first organization with which we as individuals must negotiate. The centrality of dependency for religious organizations is explicitly acknowledged by their affirmation of belief in a transcendent being—God. Whatever else churches may attempt, if they reject this task of representing dependency they are likely to become redundant. But in complex Western societies, it is unlikely that churches are the only institution to deal with dependency needs. In a pluralistic society, every institution may need to recognize that it functions with and on behalf of others in relation to issues of dependency. We began to see this, for example, in our study of a psychiatric unit.

Dependency is difficult to manage, particularly given its connection with irrational behavior. Religious institutions offer a means for addressing this connection. On the one hand, they deliberately acknowledge dependency through belief in God, acts of worship, and pastoral activity. On the other, they provide a primary means of acknowledging irrational aspects of daily life without assuming that these aspects are pathological. The arts perhaps perform a similar function, and the intimate historical links between art and religion are well known.

Dependency in adults can be difficult to face. Even the language used can appear pejorative. For an adult to be described as "dependent" can be seen as a moral judgment, as we saw in chapter 10, in the hospital staff's initial devaluation of its learning needs. Whenever we encounter dependency, we confront a primitive aspect of ourselves.

But in addition to affirming dependency, all forms of religious belief and practice also deal with emotions such as fear, love, anxiety, and guilt. Each of these emotions represents an aspect of the normal human condition as well as a possible motivation for irrational behavior. They are double-edged: without such feelings, we are not human; because of uch feelings, we may become lost. Dependency is similarly double-edged: cknowledging our dependency and working with it are the marks of uman maturity; but being dependent (immature, we sometimes call it) uns the risk of destroying those aspects of autonomy that allow us to be reative.

Our hypothesis is that the social task of religious institutions is to nable individuals to face the connections between dependency and irra- onality by providing a managed and contained context for both. This ask can be used as a model for understanding how institutions can york with those projections that they must contain on behalf of others, or we believe other social institutions have similar tasks in relation to ther human needs. Our institutions are our familiar places. But if they o not provide a secure holding environment, individuals can feel lost ithin them.

A SOCIAL HOLDING ENVIRONMENT

We emphasized the significance of a holding environment both 1 discussing the family and later when we considered organizations. eligious institutions also contribute to the creation of a holding envi- onment in society. As we have seen, a holding environment includes ontaining aggression and sexuality, providing for safe regression, and stablishing empathic connection. All these needs can be addressed 1rough ritualized symbolic structures that enable chaotic experience to e faced. Our proposition is that a key holding environment is continu- lly being negotiated and created through the unconscious interaction etween members of a society and its religious institutions.

In chapter 11, we described a setting in which joint interpretation ould be discovered. In our consultation to the law firm, we needed to rovide a kind of contained regression within which both previously nbearable feelings and centrally important beliefs and values could be rasped.

In a similar manner, religious institutions, through their use of ritual nd symbols, may facilitate a contained and managed regression for indi- iduals and for larger groups to enable them to deal with problematic eelings and experiences in a constructive rather than chaotic manner. 1deed, it may be that both the activity of church members and the nconscious relatedness of those in the outside world to religious insti- 1tions may facilitate a general social regression in the service of a soci- ty's survival and development. Two aspects of religious institutions contribute to their ability to create this holding environment: affirming the transitions of life and providing rituals for public ceremonies.

Affirming the Transitions of Life

Religious institutions represent competent management, or at least affirmation, of the ultimate boundaries to life. Obviously, the notion of God itself represents one such ultimate boundary. Moreover, religions are usually invoked at least to manage entry into the world and exit from it.

The process of living may be thought of as a series of transitions from one state to another. Some of these transitions are traditionally marked by rituals, which are not the sole prerogative of religion but which are certainly sustained by it. Rituals are means of linking the present to the past, the individual to his or her cultural heritage, and making conscious in a structured environment aspects of both individual and social life. For instance, birth, adolescence, marriage, and death are major transitions that may be marked by religious rituals. Most religions seem to be involved through rites such as baptism or circumcision, confirmation or bar mitzvah, weddings and funerals.

The popular religiosity of such rituals as christenings, weddings, and funerals remains problematic for churches. Even those who do not attend regularly turn to "their" church on these occasions. But these rituals are not merely manifestations of individual preference or belief; they have a dimension that involves groups other than those who directly take part. They have a public and social nature that requires interpretation. We suggest that religious institutions, when performing these religious tasks, can be regarded as providing a facilitating environment for constructive regression, which furthers the development both of the participants and of others (Carr 1985a).

Without some such interpretation, the tendency to look to religious ritual to celebrate these transitions seems like another instance of pervasive dependency. But that view ignores the complexity of the process. The behavior is not merely dependent; it is also irrational (for example, nonbelievers swearing their faith at a wedding ritual). People find themselves able to acknowledge their irrationality and yet persist in it. Some explanation of this behavior is, therefore, crucial.

Providing Rituals for Public Ceremonies

The corporate aspects of ritual emerge in public religious events that concern the general public, believers and nonbelievers alike

As we have indicated, these are frequently linked to ultimate issues, especially death. Some funerals and memorial services are as much facets of national life as rituals for the deceased person. The funeral of President John F. Kennedy was one such instance. Occasionally, the underlying dissension within a nation will be exposed through such a ritual.

After the British campaign in the Falkland Islands in response to the Argentinian invasion in 1982, the Prime Minister and government of Great Britain wanted a national celebration, including a service of thanksgiving for victory in St. Paul's Cathedral. The Dean, who is in charge of the cathedral, and the Archbishop of Canterbury, who is the leader of the Church of England, were responsible for arranging this celebration. Together they devised and led a worship service in which they tried to handle both the ambivalence that prevailed in the nation as a whole about having been involved in such a war and the emotions of those who had been bereaved. This religious ritual was not merely the vehicle through which feelings could be acknowledged. It was itself also an interpretation. The form of service and the sermon preached linked the conflicting emotions (rage, grief, jubilation, horror, vindictiveness) that were felt by different groups in the nation and explicitly refrained from endorsing the government's somewhat simplistic notion of victory. This interpretation was offered by the only people who could be "heard" at that moment and accepted as authoritative, because it rightly unified the complexity of the national response. Through ritual, this interpretation helped to manage diverse aspects of a dependent need to connect to something larger than the self at a time of stress.

A religious institution, therefore, may hold for a wide clientele, certainly larger than it knows, the idea that profound and incomprehensible experience which puts people in touch with their unconscious selves requires interpretation. Because such institutions stand for the seriousness of the issues marked by ritual, they sanction that experience and with their own idiosyncratic rituals offer a contained place for people's emotions. And, as in the Falklands story, from time to time such institutions may be used to articulate what others cannot express.

As the bearers and performers of ritual, religious institutions represent the spiritual dimension of life that can be profoundly disturbing when it emerges. As a consequence, an ambivalence about these institutions remains in our contemporary societies that cannot be resolved.

ILLUSION AND DELUSION

Throughout this book we have sought to identify and examine the social spaces within which individuals develop and which ultimately become part of their internal world. One such area, which offers the potential for both creative and destructive development, lies between illusion and delusion. "Illusion" refers to the normal range of fantasies through which human beings live their everyday lives. These are explorable and testable with others. In contrast, "delusion" is a pathological state in which a person constructs an idiosyncratic, untestable world in which to live. One of the characteristics of religious belief is that it specifically addresses the problematic area where illusion meets delusion (Winnicott 1951; Meissner 1984; Carr 1989).

This intersection between illusion and delusion, however, does not merely exist within an individual. It also has a social dimension. Religious institutions, like other organizations and the family, interact with their contexts more profoundly than may ordinarily be recognized. Such interaction may be easily acknowledged in theory but it may be difficult to face in practice. The internal dynamics can sometimes be appreciated, but the contextual dynamics often seem either incredible or bewildering. But, as we have been arguing, it is precisely this area of thinking that needs to be addressed and interpreted in our complex societies.

Evidence for this interaction is readily available. Changes in the beliefs or practices of religious institutions seem to have repercussions beyond those immediately affecting their adherents. When, for instance, the Church of England produced a new Prayer Book in 1980 (the first since 1662, apart from a minor revision in 1928), people from all walks of life, some of them explicitly affirming their atheism and many their agnosticism, signed petitions against it. The decision to revise the prayer book was aggressively questioned in Parliament. The more literate produced a book of essays on why the Church of England should not create new forms of liturgy, especially for those who do not attend. This discontent was expressed locally in many parishes, as nonmembers as well as members of congregations behaved in similar fashion. At the level of everyday parochial work, clergy often reported irrational behavior, usually connected with dependency, from those who had no apparent intention of joining the congregation.

At a profoundly unconscious level, people's dependence on the old prayer book was being challenged and, as usual when this happens, rage ensued. But this anger was difficult to express since it was accompanie by guilt at not believing or not attending church. This guilt was then projected not onto God, which would have been far too risky, but onto the church, especially its public representatives—bishops, clergy, and the synod.

Ministers from the United States and elsewhere tell similar stories, with appropriate cultural adjustments. For example, in the United States nonbelievers regularly decry the conversion of unused churches into condominiums or stores. People who assert that they are not religious and wish to have nothing to do with the churches, at the same time make forceful, irrational demands upon the clergy.

Behavior that would be considered bizarre elsewhere may be accepted as legitimate in churches. For instance, people may lose their wits. Churches do not have an explanation for irrational behavior, although the dependency needs they fulfill sometimes lead people to look to their clergy for explanations. But churches do appear to have an interpretive function, which can provide individuals and various groups with a focus for projecting the irrational parts of themselves. And experience suggests that these irrational aspects of behavior emerge from very deep within the self, from an area where the difference between illusion and delusion is often difficult to discern.

This observation may provide us with the link between irrationality and dependency that ensures the continuance of religious institutions. For individuals and for competing groups within a society, religious institutions keep alive the ultimate illusion—the notion of God—which is used to contain destructive aggression. Churches themselves do not contain illusions; instead what they profess, namely God, has that function. And, as we have suggested, in this area there is a double opportunity for irrationality to emerge. On the one hand, the individual experiences internal pressure and conflict in his need for an object on which to depend. On the other hand, the prevailing assumption that belief in God is a delusion or a sign of madness brings pressure from without. Inevitably much of this irrationality will simply be projected onto the church and abandoned. But by acknowledging such projections, churches can interpret some of them, and in so doing make significant statements about human beings and their life in the world.

There is also a corporate dimension to this. Institutions are not solely repositories for the projections of individuals; they can function as large-scale containers of projections from society. When corporate madness appears in a nation, for instance, the institutions that publicly embody rationality (for example, universities) may prove incapable of coherent response. If irrationality manifested in corporate form is to be recognized, it must first be acknowledged or at least demythologized in some secure place. Those connected with religious institutions, because they are unafraid of myths, can demythologize most effectively. The confrontation of the government led by religious people in present-day South Africa is an example of this.

This is not to suggest that religious people and churches somehow always get it right—to assume that they do is merely a further manifestation of dependency. But by their stance toward another world—God, life after death, a spiritual dimension to existence—religious institutions do represent a major area of human life that many feel is irrational. Yet, despite this irrationality, religious feeling wells up from the depths of being in individuals and societies in surprising fashion. And religious institutions can be used by individuals, groups, and institutions for constructively exploring their own irrationalities, if they do not deny the existence of these irrational elements. In other words, we might say that if a society is sinking into corporate *delusion* (for example, "The Jews are destroying society"), the power of affirmed *illusion* (for example, "We are all children of God"), as offered by religious bodies, may become more necessary. People live on the borders of destructive delusion and hopeful illusion. By managing this boundary, religious institutions may allow a broader range of individual experiences to be recognized, acknowledged, and ultimately brought into the interpretive stance for shared interpretation. For example, even the notion of God, as it is negotiated by individuals and groups in and around religious institutions, assists individuals in managing their experiences of dependency and irrationality by accepting something larger than themselves. The notion of God is more than a projection when it is negotiated between people and not simply asserted—it is a containing structure.

THE PERSISTENT SIGNIFICANCE OF IRRATIONALITY

In the life of the individual, there is a need for dependenc
ot handled effectively, can produce both individual and soci
Irrationality, too, requires acknowledgment and not denial. Ou
osition brings these two issues together in the context of soci
s in general.
tions function responsibly, mature personal development ar
havior on behalf of one another in society result. If, on t
, there is unmanaged and uninterpreted confusion about t

meaning of the institutional context (as in our opening story about the trustees and the hospital), then individuals may lose touch with their roles and the values these roles represent and will become lost in familiar places.

In this secular age, people tend to be cautious of acknowledging their interest or belief in anything transcendent because of the prevailing assumption that to do so is a sign of weakness or instability. Questions about death, values, ultimate meaning, the unexpected need for and response to ritual, and the persistence of imagination, artistry, and religion cannot be divorced from interpretations of dependency and irrationality.

The reason for this is that religious institutions—perhaps all institutions—are dealing simultaneously with three interconnected phenomena, each of which is vital for our age. First, belief is a distinctive aspect both of one's self image and of every commitment one makes to others. Belief has emerged as a phenomenon in each organization studied in this book. In the psychiatric unit, staff commitment to and belief in the treatment task tied them closely to one another; in the law firm, lawyers' belief in the importance of a medium-sized firm that valued the individual sustained them through a crisis around survival.

Second, religious institutions usually handle group phenomena on a large scale. They deal with large groups, both actual and in the mind—extended families, the congregation, the community, the national religious institution, other religions. Because of their complexity and lack of structure, large groups are notoriously confusing and at times bizarre. We should, therefore, expect irrational behavior to predominate in such institutions. Without irrationality, religious institutions would not exist, but without the interpretive struggle, they would lack raison d'etre. But, as we have repeatedly suggested, this is not simply an issue for religious institutions: they address it publicly on behalf of others. It is possible that others could learn from the experience of religious institutions in this area. Then the dynamic network of institutions could be mobilized for some sort of useful activity.

Third, religious institutions specifically involve commitment. Dominated as we are in this age by largely unexamined assumptions about individual autonomy, commitment can be difficult to acknowledge and even more difficult to deal with. But whether or not an individual accepts the beliefs and interpretations offered by religious organizations, commitment to something larger than the self—an institution, a community, a task—may provide sufficient containment for the interpretation of dependency and irrationality to occur.

This interpretation of religious bodies can serve as a paradigm for thinking about institutions in general. There appears to be a network of institutions that provide the holding environment for contemporary living—part of which is provided through ritual. It is possibly because this dimension of their existence has not yet been recognized by their leaders and members that our institutions are at present in turbulence and confusion, and individuals, feeling lost, are behaving increasingly irrationally. In fact, it may be that there is a degree of certainty manifested by many institutions about their tasks which is comparable to the excessive certainty we described in chapter 1 in relation to the family. In the family, members' certainty about each other leads to an inability to accept new information. In contemporary society it may be that some institutional tasks similarly need to be discovered, not assumed. We suggest that religious institutions, with their capacity to affirm both dependent and irrational aspects of normal behavior, may offer a paradigm. For they seem not only to contribute to the lives of individuals who associate with them but also to be able to discern their impact institutionally in a wider setting. In so doing they may be used to indicate the need for every institution to recognize that it exists dynamically in relation to a larger sustaining holding environment for men and women.

We are all necessarily dependent in our origins: not one of us chose to exist—we are each created by others. Any rights by which we assert our autonomy are primarily assigned to us rather than possessed by us. Furthermore, since the irrational parts of ourselves are integral to our normal everyday existence, responsible behavior means taking into account the whole range of ourselves, not only the sophisticated and rational parts. One is not preferable to the other; rationality and irrationality are complementary aspects of the human being. If either is denied, we are truly lost, and uninterpretable behavior is likely to ensue.

14 ○ Society,

Institutions,

and the Individual

This final chapter is necessarily more speculative. It is difficult enough, as we have seen, to adopt the interpretive stance and to assemble the necessary data concerning the individual and his relatedness to the small and large contexts in which he lives. Yet this effort appears simple in comparison to an examination of the problematic role of citizen and its relatedness to the vast conglomerations of society or the nation. But the uninterpreted space that is experienced between the individual and his social context is one of the main reasons for the experience of being lost. We cannot, therefore, conclude without exploring this issue.

FROM GROUP TO SOCIETY

A primary source of data about group and larger social processes is the "group relations conference," which was initially designed by researchers from the Tavistock Institute for Human Relations in London and developed in the United States by the A. K. Rice Institute and by other organizations around the world. The conference brings together people from all walks of life to study and explore authority relations in groups and organizations. In relatively unstructured small-group, large-group, and intergroup settings, the members study group behavior with the help of consultants. A simple framework is provided within which members and staff together create a temporary organization that they can study (Rice 1966).

The whole enterprise sounds somewhat removed from real life. But participants in such a social laboratory are often amazed (and sometimes dismayed) by the uncanny clarity with which familiar national or international stereotypes and behavioral characteristics appear. In the hectic effort to develop a temporary organization, businessmen become disorganized; clergy are seen as believers, yet find themselves confronting their unbelief; and psychiatrists become irrational. Sometimes more serious and terrifying things happen: members act like terrorists, women or minorities are victimized, or staff display totalitarian tendencies. When the initial amazement has past, a basic question remains: what is the reason for the rapid emergence in a group of strangers of such powerful societal manifestations? And how do we interpret these phenomena, moving from a study of individuals with their experiences, through the maze of interconnections of life, past and present, to a grasp of the components of the role of citizen?

Parallels between the dynamics of the individual and those of the small group are not difficult to find (Bion 1961; Grinberg 1985). Some of these parallels were discussed in our examination of the family. The shift to the large group, however, introduces new and different phenomena that can serve as a model of social process. By "large group" we mean one bigger than any single participant can comprehend at a glance. Such unstructured groups, in many ways comparable to mobs, are part of the experience of group relations conferences. The membership of such groups is vast; the dominant feeling is of being in a mob as dimly perceived subgroups appear, reform, and disappear, often with bewildering rapidity. The individual feels isolated, unable or unwilling to participate, desperately searching for any form of connection. Personal boundaries and identity seem to become fragile or even dissolve as each person finds difficulty maintaining psychological distance from what is happening in the group. Individuals cannot be recognized; experiences cannot be grasped; even the notion of the group itself and its task are easily lost. The world as known and trusted can feel as though it has permanently disintegrated into a series of unrelated fragments. Not surprisingly, extremes of irrationality may appear, producing the pressures of a mob and bizarre behavior, often accompanied by imminent psychological violence to the self or others (Turquet 1975).

No unstructured group can remain intact for very long; when a group lacks social cohesion, it does not provide sufficient space and opportunity for individual integration. As a result, shared defenses are unconsciously erected to protect the group and its members from the experience of chaos. The simplest and, in light of our discussion of projection, the most obvious group defense is to generate a series of polarities. Subgroups are identified and members join them in order to establish some form of identity. These subgroups become the focus for stereotyped projections. As soon as one element appears to be becoming dominant, its polar opposite arises and neutralizes it: black/white, male/female, young/old, and in a group using a consultant to examine itself, consultant/member. Some kind of stability is achieved by the group as a whole, partly due to the balance of these polarities but also partly because each subgroup is composed of familiar elements. If a member defines himself as a black or a man, at least he has a recognizable identity in the group. In the contemporary world such divisions of race, gender, and authority evoke familiar and strong feelings. Any effort to explore the underlying dynamics behind the pressured need to create such stereotyped groups is often washed away in floods of socially legitimate, and therefore unquestionable and uninterpreted, pronouncements.

When the chaos persists, a second defense may be erected: the group institutionalizes itself. Instead of personal attributes (sex, race, age) onto which projections may confidently be directed, roles become prominent and formalized. For example, consultants are not heard as potentially useful colleagues in a shared investigation but are invited to become managers of the event. Or those with assertive voices become gurus. Tradition (what is believed ought to happen) and conservatism (the avoidance of new risks) triumph. By institutionalizing itself in this fashion, a large group may believe that it will survive its own inherent destructiveness. But it does so at a cost to the individual, who begins to lose his distinctiveness. Individuals become more a role than a person; they find themselves in an institution that they have not created and to which they do not feel committed. Each individual is either lost in the chaos of the group or institutionalized into subgroups and into limiting and limited roles, and thus depersonalized. In this setting, leadership rapidly becomes stereotyped and dull, and the leader's mediating function of enabling work to develop diminishes, producing further frustration.

The process of institutionalization, therefore, carries penalties. However, provided that such institutionalizing is a temporary phase, it makes a useful contribution to the group's developing life just as the creation of polarized subgroups does. For in the swirling here-and-now dynamics of the large group these phases provide valuable plateaus between the individuals' feeling lost and isolated and the group's engaging in creative interaction. This temporary security and momentary respite contributes significantly to the group's developing life.

In our effort to link ideas about society, institutions, and the individual two points need noting. First, the process is not formal or structured. It is not a dynamic of individuals; certain members of the group do not impose it on others. It is a dynamic phenomenon of the group itself, through which certain functions for both group and individual are performed. By it, individuals and subgroups in the maelstrom of the large setting can try to position themselves in a daunting world that feels incomprehensible. Second, the conditions for communication are generated by creating the idea of some sort of institutional structure (that is, individuals are given roles on behalf of others)—however unreal in formal terms. In the disorientation produced by the large group, individuals may no longer derive their sense of themselves from within—indeed, they may often feel lost within themselves. In this chaotic setting, people may more readily orient themselves by consciously attending to something outside. As Turquet (1974) puts it, the sense of the self begins to be formed "at the skin of the other," whether this be another person, a subgroup, or just some notion in the mind of leadership, role, organizational structure, or task that can be tested in collaboration with others.

INSTITUTIONS IN SOCIETY

We suggest that this study of the dynamics of the developing large group might offer a way of thinking about some of the unconscious dynamics of the major large group in most people's lives—society. First, the experience of the larger society is often managed by similar polarities around which shared fantasies coalesce: east/west; black/white; male/female; rich/poor. These polarities serve to protect the individual from unmanageable complexity and provide a way to focus anxiety, aggression, alienation, and other unmanageable feelings derived from the chaos of living in society.

Second, institutionalization is a phenomenon of society. In many contemporary institutions, individuals encounter similar frustrations, stereotyped roles, and mediocrity as in the institutionalizing phase of the developing large group. In such a context, the individual may feel profoundly lost in relation to the larger world. In order to begin to make connections and interpret this experience, he has to manage the huge space between himself and the highly significant, but undefined, notion of society in such a way that there can be a definable and graspable interface between them. The defenses we have outlined provide a respite from the stress of this complexity but do not themselves lead to the discovery of new connections. Since institutions occupy this space between the individual and the unencompassable "society," we propose that they be used as channels for making interpretive connections. We are so preoccupied today with institutions and their visible functioning that we may overlook their importance as fantasized and experienced places in the mind, potentially usable by the individual in order to find himself in the larger world.

We suggest that a society's institutions—businesses, universities, families, presidents, corporations and so on—are significant repositories for the projections both of individuals and of various groupings. As such, they enable people to develop and sustain ideas in the mind that are essential if people are to find a way to negotiate the space between their individuality and their social context. Rather than being deadening refuges from the chaotic experience of being in the world, institutions potentially offer a means by which we may manage in a controlled fashion our inevitable regressions in the face of the imminent and threatening power that society represents. If attended to, this creation of such "institutions-in-the-mind" can be a positive means by which a person may be enabled maturely to assume his demanding range of roles in society.

There is a prevailing nervousness about institutions. They are often contrasted unfavorably with individuals and their believed personal autonomy and quest for personal meaning. Institutions can and do on occasion obstruct personal development. But that should not blind us to their potential to enhance the creative functioning of individuals. A brief and oversimplified example may serve to clarify the point.

A man may be both a father and a business executive. Each of these roles is demanding, requiring great expenditures of energy. The individual is stretched in both roles. We have discussed how the shape and function of the family appear to be changing. Parenthood is consequently a problematic role. In a tumultuous environment, business and the role of the executive are both increasingly stressful. In each role, father and executive, the individual is pressured by societal forces. If he is to be competent in either role, he needs to be able to broaden his application of certain aspects of himself, which may be mobilized in one role, in order to invest in the other. So, for example, he may need for a time to allow his executive concern with the developing future of his company to broaden into a metaphor to aid him in nurturing his children's development. Or he may similarly need to draw on his paternal concerns at home in order to grasp the regressive behavior of colleagues at work. To undertake this kind of temporary but necessary metaphoric regression in a controlled and therefore creative manner, he needs to rely on an institution-in-the-mind—in this case, the family or the company—within which to focus his experiences. This may leave him freer to acknowledge them and so to work with their implications for himself and others in the other role.

For example, as he teaches his child to ride a bicycle, he may for the first time creatively link this experience to "the company" and conceive of the company as a place where younger people can learn new skills. Or, as he gets impatient with his "childlike" subordinates at work, he may find himself thinking in a new way of his family as an organization where things must get accomplished under pressure, realizing that in the family, too, unbearable stresses might be placed on his children. We are here returning to our notion of relatedness to structures in the mind that are beyond actual experience but serve as containers for diverse feelings and ideas.

Individuals need institutions and some image of them in the mind to contain, define, and shape the space in which they operate. The more confidently people can shape this space in the complexity of their many roles (and for simplicity we have only sketchily outlined two), the more able they will be to assume other responsibilities in a range of other roles. Through these connections, individuals can become not isolated, nor depersonalized and institutionalized beings, but citizens—aware of and working with their social contexts as they interpret their experiences in related institutional roles.

To put it simply, as Joe Smith, a person, I do not have a well-defined connection to society. In my role as father in the Smith family, however, I can relate aspects of my experience to the problems of schools, real estate, and savings institutions; and my role as a mechanic in the Ford Motor Company allows me to grasp issues about unions, management, Congress, and international trade. These roles within institutions —related to institutional tasks—begin to enable the individual to establish sufficient self-definition to be able to examine and then competently assume the necessary range of social roles within society.

DEPENDENCY AND SOCIAL DYNAMICS

The forces that interfere with individuals' capacities to assume such an interpretive stance include the prevalence of social passivity in Western society. Within our institutions, individuals often feel increasingly alone and incompetent, at the mercy of seemingly uncontrollable and incomprehensible forces. The idea of an institution may provide enough fantasized security within a dependent culture for people to feel competent enough to work. But the dependent longing for a reliable institution itself tends to encourage a powerful wish for such institutions to be permanent and unchanging. These wishes, when mobilized by large groups of individuals both within and outside of institutions, contribute to institutional inflexibility in the face of social change. The social need for constancy may be seen, for example, in the anxiety that is generated when dependency-bearing institutions within a society, such as the family, medicine, and religion, change and thus begin to feel unreliable (Lawrence, ed. 1979).

In our section on the family, we discussed the power of dependency. But although dependency is central to institutional life, its use to explain complex social phenomena is limited. The idea of dependency itself seems to imply a society we do not know. When dependency provides the structural base for a society, the culture should feel unified and coherent, with certain dependable foci—president, king, or, behind these, God.

But this is not our contemporary social experience. There is little, if any, sense of an agreed upon and accepted ultimate boundary that can define and contain the varied elements of society in some form of coherence. Acceptable tradition and generally agreed upon areas of authoritative action are almost impossible to find. Instead, individuals present themselves as highly autonomous, sometimes anarchic; interest groups form themselves around causes, both real and imaginary. The wish for a unifying dependency often gives way to what appears as a series of attempted pairings between polarized groups. Groups and individuals are rapidly thrust together in the hope that they might produce something creative. The transient enthusiasm in the late 1980s about the possibility of U.S.-Soviet collaboration is one example. But these hopes are usually illusory, and the destructiveness caused by those polarities with which we are familiar today (Arabs/Jews; blacks/whites; men/women) follows. Dependency, therefore, does not seem to be the dominant dynamic when we think about social passivity in today's pluralist societies, except insofar as this pressure to pair is an intensified form of dependency.

Pierre Turquet (1974) suggested that a fourth basic assumption —which he called "oneness"—might be added to Bion's initial three. This assumption was discerned "when members [of a group] seek to join in a [fantasy of a] powerful union with an omnipotent force, unattainably high, to surrender the self for passive participation and thereby feel Existence, Well-being, and Wholeness" (p. 357). This description seems to us to be of a further stage of regression—beyond dependency—back to existence itself.

A crucial issue for our pluralistic societies is pairing, a specific form of dependency: given our complexity, can two institutions, two groups, two cultures, two races, two genders, or even two people be united to create something new, strong, and hopeful? Any pair also possesses the potential for destruction as well as creation. In a group setting, for instance, the fantasy of a competent and idealized pair is sustained by others at the cost of the loss (through projection) of their own potency. Hence when the pair fails to live up to these impossible expectations, angry but resigned reversion to passive dependency is a common response. In the life of a group this is familiar; it can be experienced, perceived, and interpreted. But in the case of a pluralist society a similar reversion to passivity cannot easily occur. For this type of society is already marked by the autonomy and individuality of its citizens and their groupings. In such a context, dependent connections to others are given limited value and when expressed, inevitably prove inadequate as the dynamic that holds things together. A society in which reliable interdependency cannot be managed may regress into a shared fantasy of oneness—the most deeply irrational loss of the self in a fusion with others. This regression —when not managed in a specifically religious context—then shows itself as social passivity.

We suggest that the customary formulations about the dependency behind social passivity are inadequate to address society's complexity. Stasis and pressure toward linking—oneness and pairing—are both intimately connected with social passivity. But by distinguishing them we create a basis upon which to attempt an interpretation that brings together the experience of individuals, the fact of the existence of institutions, and the vast notion of society, which impinges on both.

When one of the three familiar basic assumptions prevails, creative activity becomes possible as realities are tested. So, for instance, the fight/flight dynamic can usefully be mobilized for creative action in response to external threats; dependency can be useful in relation to following genuine dependable leadership; and pairing can bring together real differentiated competences. By these means the irrational parts of ourselves are harnessed to the rational. Any similar move from the more profound dynamic of oneness, however, requires an additional interim step. Since oneness involves the complete surrender of the self and a consequent loss of individual experience and therefore of the interpretive stance, active work must be carried out to overcome the stasis. Recognizing our essential interdependency, we have first to integrate the unconscious and deeply primitive parts of ourselves with the more conscious irrational parts, in order to join these with our rational selves. This allows individual interpretation to include the memory of oneness and therefore the experience of transcendent connectedness.

Because the primary and most prevalent of the first three basic assumptions is dependency, it is toward dependency that the shift from the stasis of oneness occurs. Turquet hints at this dynamic when he links oneness with "existence or the mysteries." Those institutions that affirm existence for its own sake or speak most easily in terms of mysteries —that is, chiefly but not exclusively religious organizations—are precisely those that are customarily also invited to handle dependency. The handling of dependency appears to be the crucial skill at which institutions in a pluralist society need to be adept. The move from oneness, which is utterly stultifying for individuality, into a more manageable form of dependency, therefore, comes about as individuals recognize that the profundities of existence can be named and then made available for exploration.

This formulation has its correlates in individual development, upon which we have based our argument throughout. As infants we cannot exist without our caretakers; our psychological development begins from a state of fusion. But the child's ultimate recognition of the separate existence of the other allows the capacity for negotiated interdependency and competent work to develop.

INSTITUTIONS, PROJECTIONS, AND RITUAL

A key ingredient in the process of naming and exploring this collective fantasy of oneness is the use of ritual. As we described in chapter 13, ritual provides a context within which important issues can be taken seriously; it provides space and the symbols necessary for containing diverse feelings; and it allows for the possibility of individual regression that leads to the uncovering of transcendent connections. Ritual enables people to acknowledge with others the possibility of mystery—of something unknown and larger than the self. This allows a shift out of an isolated individual fantasy of oneness to a negotiated interdependency, and makes further work possible on the nature of that dependency. Though churches and other religious organizations may stand for the significance of this larger dimension to human life, working on the nature of interdependency will be part of the task of many, if not all, institutions.

We are familiar with the pervasive presence in our society of diverse rituals. Political and public social rituals abound. Presidents and prime ministers handle ritual and dependency in their roles, as do medical, military, and sporting institutions. All institutions can provide semi-ritualized environments in which individuals may safely regress to interdependency. This regression occurs because of the meaning given to these institutions by the projections of individuals. For example, a church is perceived to be about spirituality, a hospital about being taken care of. Institutions, like individuals, exist within and contribute to a sea of projections. They are likely to be particularly susceptible to some of these, which they may be able to discern. By being thus aware of and sensitive to the projections within their environment, they may better contribute to the way in which the space between individual self-awareness and a sense of the incomprehensible "other" of society can be acknowledged and so negotiated. Institutions, therefore, are not to be compared or contrasted unfavorably with individuals, as is still done today in terms of the autonomy of the individual and the dangers of institutionalization. They are contributory components in the network of society, which generates both individual and social welfare.

Moreover, that dependency about which people tend to be wary turns out to be an important ingredient in social structures and their development. When interpreted, dependency emerges as a crucial mediating stage between the disenabling passivity of oneness and the collaborative and creative activity that comes from cooperative interaction.

The interpretable framework provided by institutions-in-the-mind that are linked to experience in institutional roles is critical. How else, when a society is experienced as intractable and ungraspable, can people manage the transition from their individual isolation to the role of contributing citizen? And, from what other roles can relevant curiosity about the wider world and its issues be sustained?

These questions concern the individual profoundly; but they also lead inevitably to an examination of the way institutions function within our societies. We suggest that whatever other tasks institutions might legitimately be pursuing, they also provide a means whereby individuals can develop a negotiated interdependency with others as they take up work roles confidently for their own benefit as well as for that of society. If this interdependency is faced, we might then risk—through the use of the interpretive stance—negotiating larger interpretations of society. We may transcend our family contexts into the broader arenas of organizational and societal life. After applying the interpretive stance within institutional roles, we may then link our experiences to that which is larger and more related to our continually developing systems of transcendent beliefs and values.

Final Reflections

We began with the individual and our primary experience of organizations, the family. We then connected individuals, with their necessarily limited experiences, to the vast societies that we humans create. We wish to conclude our discussion with some examples of how individuals might conduct their own interpretations within their organizational roles as a way of dealing constructively with these connections.

In any organization, subgroups have differentiated tasks. In each subgroup, members have particular roles. These elements — tasks and roles — provide a place from which organizational and social interpretation can be undertaken. In other words, my knowledge of my body and feelings, my recognition of my role and the task of the group to which I belong, allow me to begin to interpret my experience in relation to the institutional context.

If, for example, I am a tall, white, deep-voiced man, I begin to learn over time that others may customarily see me as aggressive, powerful, and arrogant. Some of these attributions will fit with my internal experience of myself, some will not. I will gradually discover that my internal experiences of feeling small, fearful, shy, and in need of protection will not be picked up in these usual attributions. Although others' images of me do not contribute to my understanding of my own complexity nor allow others to really know me, they may be used in my efforts to interpret my organization. My first step is to accept these attributions as an institutional creation: in my role, others see me as aggressively arrogant. If I have a leadership role in an accounting subgroup in an organization, I might begin to consider why the organization chose me to assume that role. I might then ask myself why the organization needs an aggressive presentation of accounting. I might begin to connect my interpretation with my perceptions of other people and their roles and with my fantasies about other subgroups and thus begin to develop hypotheses about the institution's overall approach to its tasks. I will consider the possibility that some aspect of the organization's aggressiveness is being projected onto my accounting subgroup and begin to think about how the management might be allowing some other aspect of the institution to work more freely with, say, passivity. Such an interpretive process represents only an initial individual contribution toward a shared interpretation. To take it any further, others must agree to work on developing negotiated interpretations. And these linking ideas will be sustained if together we can discern a transcendent task for the institution.

A similar framework can facilitate interpretive links between organizations and within society as a whole. For example, in my role as parent, I may begin to worry about not providing sufficient time for my child and begin to think about my relationship to the schools that assume some of the cultural and educational tasks for my child. If I then notice that the educational system is underfinanced and that teaching is no longer a profession that is valued by society, I can begin to think about education's primary task of fostering children's development. This view brings me to related examinations of the disintegration of the family unit, social disorder, and the increased information about child abuse, all of which are aspects of contemporary society. This examination then leads me to consider society's seeming lack of concern for its future. This model allows me to bring some of the apparently disconnected parts together into a more comprehensive picture of the whole. Once embarked on that process I become more aware of my related institutional roles and able to explore what it is to be a responsible part of this social process. By exploring my institutional role in relation to a social problem, I encourage others to explore their roles, too.

In which role might I take the question of child abuse further? It began with me in my family role as father and moved to a more general notion of parenthood. The critical link now is to the role of citizen. If I wished to explore the hypothesis further, I would discuss this concern with people in related institutional roles (in schools, courts, government) and work to develop a collaborative interpretation to explain this aspect of society. It is here that responsible behavior in the role of citizen begins to emerge. How I vote and the politics I espouse become an integral part both of my personal lifestyle as a parent and of my public behavior in my role as citizen. Behavior that is informed not just by external data but by my sensitivity to my own motivations may follow.

Seen in this light, institutions have a broader significance than their members or people more generally have realized. Among their many tasks is to provide the channels through which individuals and sub-groups in a society interact and thus create the needed space between themselves as individuals and their vast contexts. One possible cause of the decline into today's apparent social passivity may be that people have not sufficiently perceived the value of the interpretive function and therefore not given it enough attention. Trusting solely in individuals and their self-understanding in the absence of attention to role context will prove inadequate for improving life. If, however, institutions are recognized as key foci for the welter of projections with which human beings live in society, then they may usefully take this into account in their self-examination and their concern with image. If they are to be the containers for projections so that individuals may assume a variety of roles within a wider range of contexts, institutions may need to attend to these projections as they develop their work within society.

For the individual in an organizational role, extrapolation from his small, limited, and fairly insignificant world to the vast issues before us and our societies is not merely legitimate or simply desirable. It is essential in our search for the missing connections behind the experience of being lost in familiar places.

Notes

INTRODUCTION

1 Throughout this book it will frequently be necessary to refer to the individual. In order to do this, gender-specific language has to be used. We shall employ the masculine or feminine pronoun to refer to both genders (unless the context clearly indicates otherwise) in order to avoid the cumbersome "his or her" usage.

CHAPTER 1

1 The quality of curiosity we are describing has its parallels in the psychoanalytic literature. Kohut (1971) describes the child's need for the parent to provide mirroring (reflecting the child's positive qualities back to him), accepting, and empathy. Winnicott (1960a) describes the child's need for the parent to validate and recognize his spontaneous gestures so that the child can learn to recognize his "true self." Kohut's description refers to parent-child interaction prior to the formation of a cohesive self, when the child needs an idealized, mirroring other who provides the child's as yet missing capabilities. With this parental response, the child first learns to recognize aspects of himself within the parent. Winnicott's description is at a later point in development. Our effort is to describe a midpoint between these two, when the mother does not know very well what the infant needs and is uncertain.

2 See Shapiro et al. 1975; Shapiro and Zinner 1976; and Berkowitz et al. 1974.

CHAPTER 2

1 The case of Sarah and her family, described in chapters 2 and 3, and was one of a series of cases treated in a program directed by Dr. Roger Shapiro in the Adult Psychiatry Branch of the National Institute of Mental Health. Aspects of these cases were initially published in a series of papers by Drs. Roger Shapiro, John Zinner, Edward Shapiro, and David Berkowitz and reprinted in Scharff 1989.

CHAPTER 3

1 "Acknowledging, bearing and putting in perspective" are the basic tasks of psychotherapy as defined by Elvin Semrad (1969).

2 "Family therapy" is a form of treatment in which the entire family meets with one or two therapists. In the course of these meetings, family interactions are explored with the therapist acting as participant-observer (see chapter 4).

CHAPTER 4

1 Individual therapy involves a one-on-one relationship between the patient and the therapist. The task of individual therapy with hospitalized patients who are also in family therapy is to help them obtain sufficient distance from their unbearable feelings to begin to think clearly about them. As the relationship grows, the patient begins to examine this developing relationship with the therapist as a way of learning about the past.

2 The irrationality of therapists is an inevitable aspect of psychotherapy. In fact, as Elvin Semrad (personal communication) noted, "Therapy can be defined as an encounter between a big mess and a bigger mess."

3 Passes are granted to patients in a mental hospital when they have improved sufficiently to leave the grounds for short periods of time.

4 Halfway houses are programs for mental patients in transition either into or out of the hospital. They are structured programs with staff present, but there is less intensive protection than in a hospital.

CHAPTER 5

1 So called "clinical approaches" to organizational dynamics have been described by Miller 1976; Lawrence 1979; Hirshhorn 1988; Berg and Smith 1985.

CHAPTER 8

1 The consultation to this program was carried out in 1986. In 1989, the research and training aspects of the program were merged into a larger psychosocial program at McLean, leaving the adolescent and family treatment unit as one of several units belonging to the larger program.

CHAPTER 9

1 See Stanton and Schwartz 1954; Jaques 1955; Main 1957; Menzies 1960; Kernberg 1980; and James 1984.

CHAPTER 10

1 We are indebted to Dr. James Krantz for this formulation.

2 This was an interesting quote to be offered to the director of an adolescent unit. It comes from Kipling's poem about growing up ("If"). The opening

and closing lines are: "If you can keep your head when all about you / Are losing theirs and blaming it on you . . . / Yours is the Earth and everything that's in it, / And—which is more—you'll be a / Man, my son!"

CHAPTER 11

1 Sometimes people speak of the psychoanalysis of groups or of organizations (de Board 1978), but this is misleading. The rapid leap from the individual and analyst to the organization and consultant is too simple.
2 This is a fictitious name.

CHAPTER 12

1 A *Vicar* is a priest who has charge of a parish. *Parish* defines a geographical area. The Church of England offers its ministry to the people within this area. It is a characteristic of this church that those who do not attend or specifically belong may still legitimately expect, and receive, its ministrations. *Congregation* refers to those people who belong to the church and regularly attend worship.

Bibliography

Barnes, G. G. 1984. *Working with Families.* London: Macmillan.

Berg, D., and Smith, K., eds. 1985. *Exploring Clinical Methods for Social Research.* Beverly Hills: Sage.

Berkowitz, D., Shapiro, R. L., Zinner, J., and Shapiro, E. R. 1974. Concurrent family treatment of narcissistic disorders in adolescence. *Int. J. Psychoanal. Psychother.* 4:379–396.

Bion, W. R. 1961. *Experiences in Groups.* London: Tavistock.

Bion, W. R. 1962. Learning from experience. In *Seven Servants.* New York: Aronson, 1977.

Carr, A. W. 1985a. *Brief Encounters: Pastoral Ministry through the Occasional Offices.* London: SPCK.

Carr, A. W. 1985b.*The Priestlike Task.* London: SPCK.

Carr, A. W. 1989. *The Pastor as Theologian: The Integration of Pastoral Ministry, Theology and Discipleship.* London: SPCK.

deBoard, R. 1978. *Psychoanalysis of Organizations: A Psychoanalytic Approach to Behavior in Groups and Organizations.* London: Tavistock.

Devereux, G. 1967. *From Anxiety to Method in the Behavioral Sciences.* New York: Humanities Press.

Freud, A. 1965. *Normality and Pathology in Childhood.* New York: Int. Univ. Press.

Freud, S. 1905. Three essays on the theory of sexuality. In *Standard Edition*, vol. 7. London: Hogarth, 1955.

Freud, S. 1921. Group psychology and the analysis of the ego. In *Standard Edition*, vol. 18. London: Hogarth, 1955.

Freud, S. 1930. Civilization and its discontents. In *Standard Edition*, vol 21. London: Hogarth, 1955.

Grinberg, L. 1962. On a specific aspect of countertransference due to the patient's projective identification. *Int. J. Psychoanal.* 43:436–440.

Grinberg, L. 1985. Bion's contribution to the understanding of the individual and the group. In *Bion and Group Psychotherapy*, ed. M. Pines. London: Routledge and Kegan Paul.

Handy, C. 1988. *The Age of Unreason.* London: Business Books.

Heiman P. 1950. On countertransference. *Int. J. Psychoanal.* 31:81–84.

Hirschhorn, L. 1988. *The Workplace Within.* Cambridge: MIT Press.

James, O. 1984. The role of the nurse-therapist relationship in the therapeutic community. *Int. Rev. Psychoanal.* 11:151–159.

Jaques, E. 1955. Social systems as a defense against persecutory and depressive anxiety. In *New Directions in Psychoanalysis.*London: Tavistock.

Kennedy, P. 1988. *The Rise and Fall of the Great Powers: Economic Change and Military Conflict from 1500 to 2000.* London: Unwin Hyman.

Kernberg, O. 1975. *Borderline Conditions and Pathological Narcissism.* New York: Aronson.

Kernberg, O. 1976. *Object Relations Theory and Clinical Psychoanalysis.* New York: Aronson.

Kernberg, O. 1977. Boundaries and structure in love relations. *J. Amer. Psychoanal. Assoc.* 20:246–266.

Kernberg, O. F. 1980. *Internal World and External Reality.* New York: Aronson.

Kets de Vries, M. F., ed. 1983. *The Irrational Executive.* New York: Int. Univ. Press.

Khaleelee, O., and Miller, E. J. 1985. Beyond the small group: Society as an intelligible field of study. In *Exploring Individual and Organizational Boundaries: A Tavistock Open Systems Approach,* ed. W. G. Lawrence. London: Wiley.

Klein, M. 1946. Notes on some schizoid mechanisms. *Int. J. Psychoanal.* 27:99–110

Klein, M. 1975. *Love, Guilt and Reparation.* New York: Delacorte.

Kolb, J. E., and Shapiro, E. R. 1982. Administrative treatment of separation issues with families of hospitalized adolescents. *Adolescent Psychiatry* 10:343–359.

Lawrence, W. G. 1979. A concept for today: The management of oneself in role. In *Exploring Individual and Organizational Boundaries,* ed. W. G. Lawrence. London: Wiley.

Lawrence, W. G., ed. 1979. *Exploring Individual and Organizational Boundaries.* London: Wiley.

Little, M. 1951. Countertransference and the patient's response to it. *Int. J. Psychoanal.* 32:32–40.

Main, T. F. 1957. The ailment. *Brit. J. Med. Psychol.* 30:129–145.

Meissner, W. W. 1984. *Psychoanalysis and Religious Experience.* New Haven: Yale University Press.

Menninger, R. W. 1985. A retrospective view of a hospital-wide group relations training program: Costs, consequences and conclusions. *Psychiatric Annals* 38:323–339.

Menzies, I. E. P. 1960. A case-study in the functioning of social systems as a defense against anxiety. *Human Relations* 13:95–121.

Miller, E. J. 1977. Organizational development and industrial democracy: A current case-study. In *Organizational Development in the UK and USA: A Joint Evaluation*, ed. C. L. Cooper. London: Macmillan.

Miller, E. J. 1979. Open systems revisited: A proposition about development and change. In *Exploring Individual and Organizational Boundaries*, ed. W. G. Lawrence. London: Wiley.

Miller, E. J. 1980. The politics of involvement. *J. Personality and Social Systems* 2:37–50.

Miller, E. J. 1989. The "Leicester" Model: Experiential study of group and organizational processes. *Tavistock Institute of Human Relations Occasional Paper No. 10*. London: Tavistock.

Miller, E. J., ed. 1976. *Task and Organization*. London: Wiley.

Miller, E. J,. and Gwynne, G. V. 1972. *A Life Apart: A Pilot Study of Residential Institutions for the Physically Handicapped and the Young Chronic Sick*. London: Tavistock.

Miller, E. J., and Rice, A. K. 1967. *Systems of Organization: The Control of Task and Sentient Boundaries*. London: Tavistock.

Modell, A. 1975. A narcissistic defense against affects and the illusion of self-sufficiency. *Int. J. Psychoanal.* 56:275–282.

Modell, A. 1985.*Psychoanalysis in a New Context*. New York: Int. Univ. Press.

Nunberg, H. 1961. *Curiosity*. New York: Int. Univ. Press.

Olenick, S. L. 1980. The gossiping psychoanalyst. *Int. Rev. Psychoanal.* 7:439–447.

Reed, B. D. 1978. *The Dynamics of Religion: Process and Movement in Christian Churches*. London: Darton, Longman and Todd.

Rice, A. K. 1966. *Learning for Leadership*. London: Tavistock.

Scharff, J. S., ed. 1989. *Foundations of Object Relations Family Therapy*. New York: Aronson.

Searles, H. F. 1979. *Countertransference*. New York: Int. Univ. Press.

Semrad, E. 1969. *Teaching Psychotherapy of Psychotic Patients*. New York: Grune and Stratton.

Shapiro, E. R. 1978a. The psychodynamics and developmental psychology of the borderline patient: A review of the literature. *Am. J. Psychiat.* 135:1305–1315.

Shapiro, E. R. 1978b. Research on family dynamics: Indications for family and individual treatment in adolescence. *Adolescent Psychiatry* 6:360–376.

Shapiro, E. R. 1982a. The holding environment and family therapy with acting out adolescents. *Int. J. Psychoanal. Psychother.* 9:209–226.

Shapiro, E. R. 1982b. On curiosity: Intrapsychic and interpersonal boundary formation in family life. *Int. J. Family Psychiatry* 3:69–89.

Shapiro, E. R. 1985. Unconscious process in an organization: A serendipitous investigation. In *Group Relations Reader II*, ed. M. Geller and A. Coleman. Washington, D.C.: A. K. Rice Institute.

Shapiro, E. R., and Kolb, J. E. 1979. Engaging the family of the hospitalized adolescent: The multiple family meeting. *Adolescent Psychiatry* 7:322–342.

Shapiro, E. R., Shapiro, R. L., Zinner, J, and Shapiro, E. R. 1979. The borderline ego and the working alliance: Indications for individual and family treatment in adolescence. *Int. J. Psychoanal.* 58:77–87.

Shapiro, E. R. Zinner, J., Shapiro, R. L., and Berkowitz, D. 1975. The influence of family experience on borderline personality development. *Int. Rev. Psychoanal.* 2:399–411.

Shapiro, R. L., and Zinner, J. 1976. Family organization and adolescent development. In *Task and Organization*, ed. E. Miller. London and New York: Wiley.

Stanton A. H., and Schwartz, M. S. 1954. *The Mental Hospital.* New York: Basic Books.

Tower, L. E. 1956. Countertransference. *J. Amer. Psychoanal. Assoc.* 4:224–255.

Turquet, P. M. 1974. Leadership: The individual and the group. In *Analysis of Groups*, ed. G. Gibbard, J.J. Hartman, and R. D. Mann. San Francisco: Jossey-Bass.

Turquet, P. M. 1975. Threats to identity in the large group. In *The Large Group: Dynamics and Therapy*, ed. L. Kreeger. London: Constable.

Winnicott, D. W. 1951. Transitional objects and transitional phenomena. In *Through Pediatrics to Psychoanalysis.* New York: Basic Books.

Winnicott, D. W. 1960a. Ego distortion in terms of the true and false self. In *The Maturational Processes and the Facilitating Environment.* New York: Int. Univ. Press, 1965.

Winnicott, D. W. 1960b. The theory of the parent infant relationship. *Int. J. Psychoanal.* 41:585–595.

Zinner, J. 1976. The implications of projective identification for marital interaction. In *Contemporary Marriage: Structure, Dynamics and Therapy*, ed. H. Grunebaum and J. Christ. Boston: Little-Brown.

Zinner, J., and Shapiro, E. R. 1975. Splitting in families of borderline adolescents. In *Borderline States in Psychiatry*, ed. J. Mack. New York: Grune and Stratton.

Zinner J., and Shapiro, R. L. 1972. Projective identification as a mode of perception and behavior in families of adolescents. *Int. J. Psychoanal.* 53:523–530.

Permissions

Clinical and case material in the following chapters has been adapted with permission from the sources indicated:

Chapter 1: Shapiro, E. R. 1982. On curiosity: Intrapsychic and interpersonal boundary formation in family life. *International Journal of Family Psychiatry* 3:77–79. Copyright © International Universities Press, Inc.

Chapter 2: Shapiro, E. R., Zinner, J., Shapiro, R. L., and Berkowitz, D. A. 1975. The influence of family experience on borderline personality development. *International Review of Psychoanalysis* 2:399–411. Copyright © Institute of Psycho-Analysis.

Chapters 3 and 4: Shapiro, E. R. 1982. The holding environment and family therapy with acting out adolescents. *International Journal of Psychoanalytic Psychotherapy* 9:209–226; Shapiro, E. R. 1978. Research on family dynamics: Clinical implications for the family of the borderline adolescent. *Adolescent Psychiatry* 6:360–376; Shapiro, E. R., Shapiro, R. L., Zinner, J., and Berkowitz, D. A. 1977. The borderline ego and the working alliance: Indications for family and individual treatment in adolescence. *International Journal of Psychoanalysis* 58:77–87. Copyright © Institute of Psycho-Analysis.

Chapter 6: Shapiro, E. R. 1985. Unconscious process in an organization: A serendipitous investigation. In *Group Relations Reader II*, ed. A. D. Colman and M. H. Geller. Washington: A. K. Rice Institute.

Chapter 8: Shapiro, E. R., and Carr, A. W. 1987. Disguised countertransference in institutions. *Psychiatry* 50:72–82.

Chapter 13: Carr, A. W. 1987. Irrationality in religion. In *Irrationality in Social and Organizational Life*, ed. J. Krantz. Washington: A. K. Rice Institute.

Final Reflections: Shapiro, E. R. 1987. Interpreting irrationality. In *Irrationality in Social and Organizational Life*, ed. J. Krantz. Washington: A. K. Rice Institute.

Index

A. K. Rice Institute, 167

Adolescence, 35; interpersonal curiosity in, 18–20

Affirmation, 4, 36, 69, 77–78, 80, 87, 142–43, 158, 160, 166

Authority: for experience, 12, 23, 118; in an institution, 98–99, 105–06, 121–22, 124–26, 135; personal, 99; consultative, 134

Basic assumptions, 68–69, 174; application to organizations, 73–74

Bion, W. R., 23, 70, 73; group theory, 67–69

Boundary: personal, 12–13, 15, 17, 18, 37; in marriage, 18–19; basis of interpretation, 20; formation in therapy, 20, 45–49; in family, 35, 37, 42; in role, 64, 72; in systems, 65; in therapeutic organizations, 72; of life, 160; of society, 173

Certainty, pathological, 14–20; and imagination, 66; about internal experience, 82; about organizational task, 166. *See also* Curiosity

Consultant, 81–82; experience of, 98–101, 134; authority of, 134

Consultation: internalized, 80–81; to a mental hospital, 97–110; internal, 123–32; about training and learning, 130–31; values and beliefs in, 133–43

Containment, 13, 36–37, 49, 59, 112, 180; in hospital, 113; through ritual, 159, 161, 164, 166. *See also* Holding

environment.

Countertransference, 66, 111–12; in institutions, 116–19; disguised, 118–19; in consultation, 134

Culture, 146, 154, 156

Curiosity: interpersonal, 11–21. *See also* Certainty

Delusion: contrasted with illusion, 162–64

Dependency: in marriage, 23; relationship between autonomy and, 26–29, 31, 33, 36, 158; denial of, 27, 33; in family, 35; as basic assumption, 68; in consultation, 100–01, 139; and learning, 131; and irrationality, 155–66; and social dynamics, 173–76

Empathy, 12, 36, 39, 48–49, 54, 82; failure of, 37, 58

Experience, individual: and boundary formation, 12; use in interpretive stance, 56–59, 62, 64, 81–85; and discerning the relevant context, 63–64, 75–76, 79–80, 154, 156, 171–72; in role, 78–80, 88–94; 127–28; 151–54; 172; and social interpretation, 178–80

Family: as first organization, 6, 11, 22, 36–37; as open system, 36, 65

Fantasy: shared unconscious, 38, 41, 43–45, 82, 170

Fight/flight: as basic assumption, 68–69; dynamic, 157; and creative action, 174–75